BIG ENGLISH 6

T0345694

Contents

Pearson Education Limited
Edinburgh Gate
Harlow
Essex CM20 2JE
England
and Associated Companies throughout the world.

www.pearsonelt.com/bigenglish

First published 2014
Seventh impression 2018

ISBN: 978-1-4479-5096-7

Set in Apex Sans
Editorial and design management by Hyphen S.A.
Printed in Slovakia by Neografia a.s.

Acknowledgements

The publisher would like to thank the following for their contributions:

Tessa Lochowski for the stories and CLIL pages.

Sagrario Salaberri for the Phonics pages.

The publisher would like to thank the following for their kind permission to reproduce their photographs:

(Key: b-bottom; c-centre; l-left; r-right; t-top)

Alamy Images: Ace Stock Limited 27cr, Allstar Picture Library 86tl, Anders Blomqvist 34, 101cl, Blend Images 34t, 54tc, Blend Images 34t, 54tc, blickwinkel 66tr, Chris Rout 22tr, Design Pics Inc 2tr, 4bl, dieKleinert 75tr, 96tr, eddie linssen 54tr, geogphotos 64cr, GL Archive 18tr, Glow Asia RF 3br, 34c, Glow Asia RF 3br, 34c, Hemis 66cl, i love images 17cr, Ilya Genkin 76cl, Image Source 12tc, Image Source Plus 87tc, INTERFOTO 92tr, Jamie Pham Photography 87tl, Jeff Morgan 14 95tr, 96bl, MBI 22c, Megapress 34r, michel platini Fernandes Borges 11tc, OJO Images Ltd 22cl, 91tc, rgbstudio 12tr, RubberBall 100cr, Sabena Jane Blackbird 66tl; **Corbis:** David Bebber / Reuters 93tr, Ian Lishman / Juice Images 2cl, KidStock / Blend Images 22cr, Ocean 2tc, Sigrid Olsson / ZenShui 35tr, Wavebreak Media Ltd / Alloy 8tr; **Datacraft Co Ltd:** 54c; **Digital Vision:** 80tr; **DK Images:** Angela Coppola 2cr, Linda Whitwam 104br; **Fotolia. com:** Andres Rodriguez 39br, CandyBox Images 35c, chawalitpix 50tl, Eléonore H 13tr, 35cr, faizzaki 60cr, feferoni 67cl, Felix Mizioznikov 22tl, fergregory 34tr, godfer 24tr, Goran Bogicevic 54tl, Iva 76, J_Foto 23c, 35tl, Kara-Kotsya 54cl, KaYann 76tl, 81c, koya979 34tc, Kzenon 86tr, michaeljung 26tr, napgalleria 34tl, PiLensPhoto 67tl, 96tl, S.White 34l, Sabphoto 12cr, Subbotina Anna 77tl, 83tr, 96cr; **Getty Images:** André De Kesel 55cr, Blend Images / Ariel Skelley 2c, Danita Delimont / Gallo Images 78tr, Fuse 2tl, 54cr, 64br, Mark Bowden 22tc, 31tc, SCIEPRO / Science Photo Library 40cr; **Glow Images:** Perspectives 12tl; **Pearson Education:** 66c, 68tr, 99tr; **PhotoDisc:** Ryan McVay 12cl; **Shutterstock.com:** Aleksandar Todorovic 76c, Anna Omelchenko 90tr, 96bc, AVAVA 21tr, Blend Images 48bl, CandyBox Images 7tr, chungking 76cr, Costazzurra 34cl, CREATISTA 48br, Dim Dimich 14tr, edg 87tr, 96br, 106tr, Edyta Pawlowska 32bl, Galina Barskaya 4cl, Giuseppe_R 48cl, Hubis 40tr, Ivaschenko Roman 82tr, Julian Rovagnati 4tl, karelnoppe 41tr, kouptsova 3bl, Matthew Jacques 76tc, milias1987 28cr, Monkey Business Images 71cr, Nella 77c, Nestor Noci 77tr, 96c, Odua Images 38cr, Oleg_Mit 38cl, Oleksiy Mark 64tr, Phon Promwisate 77tc, 96cl, photogl 12c, R. Gino Santa Maria 3cr, Robert Crum 23cr, 101tl, Ross Brown 19tr, silver-john 103tr, Slazdi 77cr, Somchai Som 77cl, 105tr, Stuart G Porter 55tr, szefei 43, Tara Flake 3cl, Tracy Whiteside 48cr; **SuperStock:** age fotostock 9tr, Fine Art Images 55br, 63tr

Cover images: *Front:* **Corbis:** Citizen Stock / Blend Images cr, Rob Lewine / Tetra Images cl, c, Westend61 r; **Shutterstock.com:** Derek Latta l

All other images © Pearson Education

Every effort has been made to trace the copyright holders and we apologise in advance for any unintentional omissions. We would be pleased to insert the appropriate acknowledgement in any subsequent edition of this publication.

Illustrated by
Q2A Media Services, Anthony Lewis

Big English Song

From the mountaintops to the bottom of the sea,
From a big blue whale to a baby bumblebee-
If you're big, if you're small, you can have it all,
And you can be anything you want to be!

It's bigger than you. It's bigger than me.
There's so much to do and there's so much to see!
The world is big and beautiful and so are we!
Think big! Dream big! Big English!

So in every land, from the desert to the sea
We can all join hands and be one big family.
If we love, if we care, we can go anywhere!
The world belongs to everyone; it's ours to share.

It's bigger than you. It's bigger than me.
There's so much to do and there's so much to see!
The world is big and beautiful and so are we!
Think big! Dream big! Big English!

It's bigger than you. It's bigger than me.
There's so much to do and there's so much to see!
The world is big and beautiful and waiting for me.
A One, two, three...
Think big! Dream big! Big English!

unit 1 ALL ABOUT SCHOOL

1 What school activities do you see in the pictures? Write the numbers.

___ going on a field trip   ___ giving a presentation

___ working on computers   ___ taking a test

___ doing a project   ___ practising yoga

2 Read and ✓. What would you like your school to have?

	lots of	some	none
1 free time	☐	☐	☐
2 homework	☐	☐	☐
3 tests	☐	☐	☐
4 group projects	☐	☐	☐
5 after-school clubs	☐	☐	☐
6 independent work	☐	☐	☐
7 field trips	☐	☐	☐
8 computers	☐	☐	☐

3 Tick (✔) the verbs you use with each phrase. Then listen and check your answers.

	do	study for	hand in	finish	take
1 a test					
2 an essay					
3 a book review					
4 homework					
5 a project					

4 Read. What should each pupil have done? Match the name to the advice. Write the letter.

I finished my essay but my puppy ate it when I wasn't looking.

Katherine

I left my book on the bus yesterday. I can't hand in my book report.

Mark

I didn't start my History project until yesterday. I couldn't finish it last night.

Tabitha

I wanted to study for the Maths test but I started playing video games. And then it was too late. My mum told me to go to bed.

Dean

___ **1** Katherine
___ **2** Mark
___ **3** Tabitha
___ **4** Dean

a should have paid attention to the time.
b should have done it again.
c should have done it earlier.
d should have been more careful.

THINK BIG

Complete the sentences with an excuse or some advice.

1 A: Ben hasn't finished his Science project because he didn't start it until last night.

B: He _____.

2 A: Rich _____.

B: He should have been more careful.

5 Listen and read. Circle T for true or F for false.

ninja_fly

Hi, everyone! What's going on? I need your advice. I've got this problem with my mum. My mum has volunteered for every dance, every field trip and every fundraising activity we've had at school so far this year. Sometimes I like it. But you know something? Children make fun of me because she's always here. It's embarrassing. I know she thinks the school needs her help but I need her help, too… to stay away. What should I do?

free_mind09

OK, ninja_fly. I understand you. It can be really annoying to have your mum at school all the time. You should tell her how you feel. Ask her to stop volunteering for everything and stop coming to school so often. Take my advice. I had the same problem with my mum and it worked for me.

2good_for_u

I agree with free_mind09. You should tell your mum that it bothers you when she comes to school so often. But I don't think she should stop volunteering. I'll bet she likes it and the school needs it. You should be glad she wants to help. You should tell her that she's a brilliant mum but that you would like her to volunteer at school less often. Think positively!

1 Ninja_fly's mum volunteers too much at his school.	**T**	**F**
2 Both free_mind09 and 2good_for_u think ninja_fly should tell his mum to stop volunteering.	**T**	**F**
3 Free_mind09 didn't have the same problem with her mum.	**T**	**F**
4 2good_for_u thinks volunteering is good.	**T**	**F**

6 Answer the question.

If your mum volunteered at your school, would you feel the same way as ninja_fly? Why/Why not?

_____

_____

7 Listen and read. Circle the correct answers.

Jim:	Hi, Ollie. Have you met the new exchange student yet?
Ollie:	No. Why?
Jim:	She's from Finland and she's really nice!
Ollie:	Nice, <u>huh</u>? Is she clever, too?
Jim:	Very clever. I've talked to her.
Ollie:	In English?
Jim:	Of course in English. But maybe I'll start learning Finnish now.
Ollie:	<u>You're crazy</u>. You haven't even learnt English yet and you *are* English.
Jim:	Finnish is different. I'm sure I'll learn it fast. I'm motivated!
Ollie:	<u>Yeah, yeah, yeah</u>.

1 Ollie **has seen / hasn't seen** the exchange student.

2 Jim **has already talked / hasn't talked** to the exchange student.

3 The exchange student **speaks / doesn't speak** English.

4 Jim **wants / doesn't want** to speak Finnish to the exchange student.

8 Look at 7. Circle the correct answers.

1 When Ollie says "Nice, huh?", "huh" means that he's:

    a not interested.   **b** interested.

2 "You're crazy" means:

    a what you're saying doesn't make any sense.   **b** what you're saying makes sense.

3 The expression "yeah, yeah, yeah" means:

    a I like what you say.   **b** I don't believe that you'll do what you say.

9 Complete the dialogues. Circle the correct expressions. Then listen and check your answers.

1 **A:** I'm going to stop playing video games forever!

    B: Huh? / You're crazy! You've played video games ever since I met you.

2 **A:** Jeffrey hasn't asked anyone to the dance yet.

    B: He hasn't, **yeah, yeah, yeah. / huh?** I wonder who he'll ask.

3 **A:** This time I'm going to hand in my project on time.

    B: You're crazy. / Yeah, yeah, yeah. That's what you always say but you're always late.

Has she **done** her solo <u>yet</u>?	Yes, she **has**. She **has** <u>already</u> **done** it.
	No, she **hasn't**. She **hasn't done** it <u>yet</u>.
Have they <u>ever</u> **won** an award?	Yes, they **have**./No, they **haven't**.

10 Read about Mike and Tom. Then write the answers or questions.

Mike and Tom's Social Science Project

 **8:45 PM** Mike and Tom are playing video games. They haven't started their Social Science project.

 **2:00 AM** Mike has finished making the model pyramid but Tom hasn't finished his research yet.

 **8:15 AM** Mike and Tom have finished their project. Tom has fallen asleep.

1 It's 8:45 p.m. Have Mike and Tom got supplies for their project yet?

_____

2 It's 8:45 p.m. Has Mike completed the model of the pyramid yet?

_____

3 It's 2:00 a.m. Has Tom started doing research on the computer yet?

_____

4 It's 2:00 a.m. Have Mike and Tom finished their project yet?

_____

5 It's 8:15 a.m. _____

Yes, they have. Mike and Tom have already arrived in the class.

6 It's 8:30 a.m. _____

Yes, they have. Mike and Tom have handed in their project.

| He **has** <u>already</u> **finished** the project. | He **finished** it <u>yesterday</u>. |
| He **hasn't finished** the project <u>yet</u>. | He **didn't finish** it <u>yesterday</u>. |

11 Look at Sarah's to-do list. Then complete the sentences.

1 Sarah _____ posters for the art exhibition at 4:00.

2 She _____ already _____ posters for the art exhibition.

3 Sarah _____ her book review at 5:30.

4 She _____ already _____ her book review.

5 Sarah _____ her Science project yet.

6 Sarah _____ her Science project tonight.

> **Things to do:**
>
> 1 Make posters for art exhibition at 4:00 ✔
>
> 2 Start book review at 5:30 ✔
>
> 3 Finish Science project tonight ☐

12 Complete the dialogues. Use the correct form of the verbs in brackets.

1 (go)

    A: Has Kathy _____ to her dancing lesson yet?

    B: Yes, she _____ to her dancing lesson at 3:00.

2 (meet)

    A: Has Mark _____ the exchange student yet?

    B: No, he _____ the exchange student yet.

3 (hand in)

    A: Has Trudy _____ her homework yet?

    B: No, she _____ her homework yet.

4 (eat)

    A: Has Sean _____ dinner yet?

    B: Yes, he _____ dinner at 6:00.

13 Complete the sentences. Circle the correct form of the verbs.

1 I **have finished / finished** my essay last night but I **haven't handed / didn't hand** it in yet.

2 Jan **has already taken / took** the test yesterday but she **has studied / didn't study** for it. She should have studied more.

3 We **haven't started / didn't start** our project yet. We **haven't had / didn't have** time yesterday.

14 Read. When do pupils in Poland start taking tests?

School in Poland

Do you like taking tests? Then you wouldn't like going to primary school in Poland. Pupils only take one official test, at the end of Year 6 and they don't get marks for the first three years of school. Would you like that? That doesn't mean that pupils don't learn. They are busy learning about many subjects. In Poland, pupils must study the following subjects: Art, modern foreign languages (like German or English), Gym (P.E.), Music, History, Civics, Science, Maths, Technology and Computer Science. They have a lot of these lessons every day. Also, each week pupils take part in various after-school activities, such as sports, theatre or computer clubs. How many subjects do you study? Has your school got any interesting after-school clubs? Have you ever joined one?

The school day is shorter in Poland, too. A typical day starts at 8:00 and finishes at 12:00 or 1:00. That gives pupils in Poland more free time than pupils in say, Spain or the UK. They don't complain about that! Would you?

15 Read 14 again and complete the sentences with the words in the box.

> daily   free time   timetable   typical

1 Most Polish pupils are happy with a shorter school day and more _____.

2 Each pupil has a lot of different lessons _____.

3 A _____ school day in Poland is 4 or 5 hours long.

4 A school _____ in Poland includes Computer Science and Civics.

16 How does school in Poland compare with your school?

1 Write one sentence about how it's different.

_____

_____

2 Write one sentence about how it's similar.

_____

_____

17 Read. How many pupils are there in an average Finnish class?

Education in Finland, China and Poland is different in some ways but pupils in all these countries do well in achievement tests. Finland has got the highest grades in Science, Maths and Reading, yet pupils go to school for only four hours a day on average. That's quite amazing! Most pupils in Poland are at school a little longer. In China, children are at school from 8 to 11 hours a day.

Class size is also different. In Finland, classes are small. The average class size is 18. Classes in Poland have got about 25 pupils. In China, they're much larger. The way the school day is structured is different, too. Pupils in China and Poland follow timetables but in Finland, pupils decide what they want to do each day. The teacher gives them choices and the pupils decide.

Pupils in these countries don't do a lot of homework. Is homework important? People have got very different opinions on this topic. The interesting thing is that pupils in these countries learn a lot without doing a lot of homework. They've got more time to enjoy learning about things outside of the classroom. Do you think that's the reason their test marks are so high?

	Finland	China	Poland
How many hours of school?	4	8–11	4–5
How large are classes?	18	37	25
Is there a timetable?	No	Yes	Yes
How much time do pupils spend doing homework each day?	half an hour daily	one hour daily	one hour daily

18 Read 17 again and circle T for true or F for false.

1 Children in China spend more time at school than children in Poland.   T   F

2 Class size is the largest in Poland.   T   F

3 Pupils in Finland have got a strict school timetable.   T   F

4 Children in Finland and Poland do a lot of homework.   T   F

 THINK BIG   If you could choose subjects to study, which would you choose? Why?

In an opinion paragraph, you share your opinion about a topic. To write an opinion paragraph, follow these steps:

- Write your opinion. Use your opinion as the title of your opinion paragraph. For example:

  Longer School Days Will Not Improve Grades

- To begin your opinion paragraph, rewrite the title of your paragraph as a question. Then answer the question with your opinion:

  Will longer school days improve grades? In my opinion, they won't.

- Next, write reasons for your opinion:

  Pupils will be too tired after a longer school day to do their homework. They'll have less time to work on school projects and study for tests.

- Then, write suggestions:

  I think offering after-school study periods for pupils who need extra help is a better idea. Teachers could also organise more group projects. That way, pupils could help each other while they complete assignments.

- Finally, write a conclusion:

  In my opinion, offering extra help to pupils and organising more group projects are better ideas than having longer school days. Longer school days might even cause pupils to get even lower grades because they'll be tired and more stressed.

19 **Choose one of the school issues below.**

- Pupils should/shouldn't use mobile phones at school.
- It's important /not important to use computers in the classroom.

State your opinion here: _____

20 **Write an outline for your topic in 19. Complete the chart below.**

Title rewritten as question:
Main opinion:
Reason:
Suggestion:
Conclusion:

21 **Write an opinion paragraph on a separate piece of paper. Use your information from 20.**

22 Read. Unscramble the questions. Use the present perfect form of the verbs. Then complete the answers.

DONE
Do my Social Science homework

Finish my Science project

Anna

NOT DONE
Study for Maths test

1 yet / Anna / do / Social Science homework

Q: _____

A: _____

2 study for / Maths test / her / she / yet

Q: _____

A: _____

3 she / finish / yet / Science project / her

Q: _____

A: _____

23 Complete the sentences. Use the correct form of the verbs in brackets.

1 Mark _____ (study) for his Maths test yesterday.

2 Sarah _____ (finish) her book report last week.

3 John _____ (hand in, not) his History assignment yet.

4 Marissa _____ already _____ (do) her homework.

24 Write the answer.

George didn't hand in his essay because he fell asleep and didn't finish it. What should he have done? Choose the best idea in the box. Add an idea of your own.

done it earlier   done it again   paid less attention to the time

_____

_____

unit 2 AMAZING YOUNG PEOPLE

1 Match the pictures to the sentences about life dreams. Write the numbers.

Someday I would like to…

☐ create a photography blog

☐ be a professional football player

☐ climb a mountain

☐ start my own band

☐ do voluntary work in Africa

☐ find a cure for diseases

2 Write down four of your dreams. Rank them by importance. 1 = most important. 4 = least important.

1 _____

2 _____

3 _____

4 _____

3 Look at 2. Which of your dreams will be the most difficult to achieve? Draw a box around it. Which dream will be the easiest to achieve? Underline it. Which dream can you achieve right now? Write it here:

_____

4 Read. Then circle T for true or F for false

My parents are amazing people! My mum's a writer. She wrote and published her first book when she was just 14 years old! She also speaks three languages: English, Spanish and French. My dad is a famous chess player. He has played chess for over 20 years and has won many tournaments. He also plays the piano and the guitar. My parents are amazing people for all their achievements – especially for being wonderful parents to me and my sister!

Our children are amazing! Our son Chris is brilliant at science. At just ten years old, he started his own science club. The club meets every Friday after school. Last week, he won an award for his latest invention: a portable mp3 case that protects your mp3 player from getting wet! He wants to be a doctor when he grows up. Emma's a terrific athlete! She's the captain of her athletics and football teams. Her football team has just won a big football tournament. Emma won the Most Valuable Player award! Emma loves being active… her biggest dream is to climb a mountain one day! We are very proud of our amazing children!

1 Chris's dad has published a book.	T	F
2 His mum speaks three languages.	T	F
3 Chris's dad plays two instruments.	T	F
4 Chris hasn't invented anything yet.	T	F
5 Emma's team has just won a football tournament.	T	F
6 Emma has already climbed a mountain.	T	F

5 Complete the sentences. Use the words in the box.

> invented something   published a book   speak 23 languages   was a contestant

1 Harry, a young boy from Hampshire, UK, _____ on a TV programme called *Junior Bake Off.* He won with his amazing carrot cake.

2 Kevin Doe _____ amazing when he was only 13. He made batteries from junk and helped bring electricity to people's homes in Sierra Leone.

3 Timothy Donor taught himself to _____ by the time he was 16.

4 Adora Svitak _____ about how to write when she was only seven.

THINK BIG   Which of the achievements in 5 do you think is the most important? Why?

6 Listen and read. Then answer the questions.

Adora Svitak

by Tracy Dorington

Adora Svitak considers herself a writer, a teacher and an activist. She began writing when she was four years old. She wrote *Flying Fingers* at age seven. In it, she talks about how important writing is and explains how to write. In 2008, Adora published a book of poetry that she co-wrote with her sister.

Adora says that when she hears children say that reading and writing aren't very important in their lives, she gets upset. She thinks that reading and writing about ideas can help change the world. In 2010, Adora gave a presentation titled *What Adults Can Learn from Kids*. She said that adults need to think like children because children think optimistically and creatively when solving problems. She mentioned children like Ruby Bridges, who helped end segregation in the United States. Adults, on the other hand, think about limitations and problems.

Adora continues to publish her work and give speeches. In 2011, she published her first full-length novel, *Yang in Disguise*. In 2012, Adora won an award given by the National Press Club. At the awards ceremony, she gave a speech about the importance of girls achieving their goals and living their dreams. One of Adora's goals is to win a Nobel Prize.

Adora believes that the way to change the world is to trust children and expect that they'll do great things at a young age. Parents and teachers, she says, have got low expectations of pupils. They don't expect children to achieve much. They expect children to listen and not show their brilliance. This thinking has to change. She says that adults should expect wonderful things and learn to listen to children. The future depends on it.

1 What's one of Adora's accomplishments?

_____

2 What's one of Adora's future goals?

_____

3 How does Adora believe the world should change?

_____

4 Do you agree or disagree with Adora? Explain your answer.

_____

7 Listen. Circle T for true or F for false.

Jen: Phil, what's your brother doing on his computer? I can see he's really <u>getting into it</u>.

Phil: He's probably working on one of his computer programs.

Jen: He writes computer programs? But he's only twelve!

Phil: I know. He started writing programs when he was about nine.

Jen: Nine? That's incredible.

Phil: He's in trouble with my parents, though. He wants to <u>drop out</u> of school and work on his programs all day.

Jen: <u>You're joking</u>, aren't you?

Phil: Yeah, I'm <u>just kidding</u>.

1 Phil's brother likes computers a lot.   T   F

2 His brother started working with computers when he was in his teens.   T   F

3 His parents don't want their children to spend all day on the computer.   T   F

4 Phil's brother is going to stop going to school.   T   F

8 Look at 7. Read the underlined expressions. Match the expressions to the meanings. Write the letter.

___**1** get into   **a** say something funny to make people laugh

___**2** drop out   **b** say something surprising that doesn't sound possible

___**3** be joking   **c** stop going before you finish

___**4** be kidding   **d** become interested in

9 Answer the questions.

1 Have you ever dropped out of anything? What was it? Why did you drop out?

_____

2 Are you getting into something interesting this year? What is it? Why do you like it?

_____

3 Look at 7. Why did Jen say, "You're joking"?

_____

How long **has** she **played** the piano?
She**'s played** the piano <u>for</u> five years.

How long **have** they **known** about William Kamkwamba?
They**'ve known** about him <u>since</u> they saw a film about him.

10 Look and match the phrases to since or for.

11 Complete the sentences with the present perfect form of the verbs and for or since.

1 Karen loves swimming. She _____ (swim) competitively _____ she was five.

2 Ray loves reading. He _____ (become) very interested in the Middle Ages _____ he read about it in Social Science.

3 Francis is taking part in a TV game show. He _____ (study) hard _____ three days.

4 Chloe loves animals. She _____ (volunteer) at the animal shelter _____ two months.

> How long **has** your brother **been playing** tennis?
> He**'s been playing** tennis <u>since</u> he was five.
>
> How long **have** you and your sister **been bungee jumping**?
> We**'ve been bungee jumping** <u>for</u> two years.

12 Read. Answer the questions. Use the present perfect continuous and the words in brackets.

Twelve-year-olds Bob and Jenny have got their own business, called 'Kids Biz'. They started working when they were nine. They do jobs like cutting the grass and washing cars. Six months ago, Jenny started babysitting, too. They also volunteer in the community. Bob started collecting money for the animal shelter two years ago. He does that every year. Jenny collects food for the homeless. She started doing that when she was 11. They both blog, too. They started blogging when they started Year 7.

1 How long have Bob and Jenny been working?

_____ (since)

2 How long has Jenny been babysitting?

_____ (for)

3 How long has Bob been volunteering for the animal shelter?

_____ (for)

4 How long has Jenny been collecting food for the homeless?

_____ (since)

5 How long have they been blogging?

_____ (since)

13 Answer the questions using complete sentences.

1 Think about something you're studying at school. How long have you been studying it?

_____

2 Think about something you love doing. How long have you been doing it?

_____

14 Match the amazing people to their accomplishments at young ages.

___ **1** Mozart, who everyone has heard of, composed

___ **2** At two years old, Aelita Andre created beautiful paintings

___ **3** Fourteen-year-old Nadia Comaneci scored a perfect 10 in gymnastics –

___ **4** A twelve-year-old boy from France changed the world of reading and writing forever

a when he invented the Braille code to help the blind read and write.

b an amazing accomplishment for such a young athlete at the Olympic Games.

c that art critics through the ages will admire.

d a symphony at four and an opera at fourteen – all by himself!

15 Unscramble the words and write the letters in the boxes. Look at the underlined words in 14 to help you. There's a message for you. Use the numbers and letters to find the message.

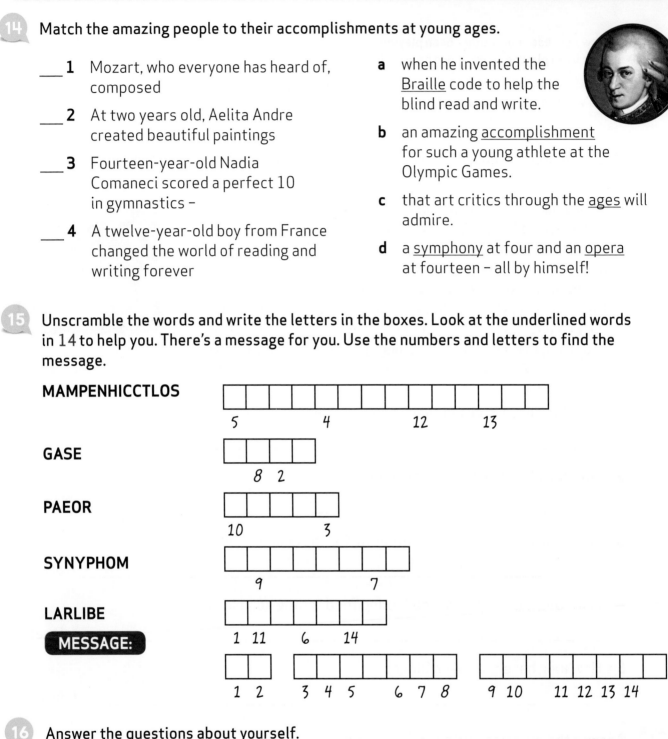

MAMPENHICCTLOS

5   4   12   13

GASE

8 2

PAEOR

10   3

SYNYPHOM

9   7

LARLIBE

MESSAGE:

1 11   6   14

1 2   3 4 5   6 7 8   9 10   11 12 13 14

16 Answer the questions about yourself.

1 Mozart composed symphonies and operas because he loved creating music. What do you like creating?

_____

2 Nadia Comaneci practised gymnastics every day and was proud of herself and her accomplishments. What accomplishments are you proud of?

_____

17 Read. When was Earthdance International founded?

Imagine a World of Peace

Conflict happens everywhere. It happens in our homes, our schools, our friendships and our world. When conflict happens, people start to 'take sides'. To *take sides* means to believe that one person, group or opinion is completely right and the others are completely wrong. When people take sides, they often don't listen to or hear the other side's concerns or opinions. Do you sometimes feel that someone isn't listening to you when you give your opinion or explain your ideas? How can you encourage people to really listen to you?

Can you imagine a world without conflict? Can you imagine a world where people live together peacefully? Earthdance International can. Earthdance International is an organisation that was founded in 1997. Its purpose is to use music and dance to bring people and countries together for peace – especially countries taking sides against each other. Once a year, Earthdance International organises the Global Festival for Peace. The Festival takes place in different countries around the world, at the same time, on the same day. It's 'the largest global synchronised music and peace event in the world'. It has taken place in over 80 countries as well as online! Musicians, singers, dancers and artists from around the world come together to create song and dance and talk about peaceful ways to end conflict, injustice and environmental problems. Everyone enjoys the music and fun but they're also hard at work discussing ways to make the world a better place. Earthdance International is committed to finding peaceful solutions to difficult problems.

18 Read 17 again and answer the questions.

1 Earthdance International invites people to get together to talk while dancing and listening to music. Why do you think the organisation believes that dancing and music are important for creating peace?

_____

_____

2 Would you like to join Earthdance International? Why/Why not?

_____

_____

THINK BIG Why do people take sides? What happens when they do?

In a biography, you write about the important events and details of someone's life. These can include:

- the place where someone was born
- the schools the person went to and what he or she studied
- the jobs the person had

- accomplishments
- important memories and people
- interests

It helps to ask questions and put the events in the correct order.

19 Unscramble the questions. Imagine you are interviewing Stephen Hillenburg, the creator of SpongeBob SquarePants.

1 born? / were / where / you

You: _____?

Stephen: I was born in Anaheim, California, in 1961.

2 what / study / you / did / at university?

You: _____?

Stephen: I studied Marine Biology at university but I really wanted to study Art.

I got a Master of Fine Arts degree in animation in 1991.

3 are / some / your / what / of / important memories?

You: _____?

Stephen: When I was young, I loved watching films about the sea. I loved drawing and painting, too.

4 jobs / have / kind of / what / you / had?

You: _____?

Stephen: I was a marine biologist from 1984 to 1987. I started working as an animator in 1991.

5 what / your / some of / are / accomplishments?

You: _____?

Stephen: I've made many films but my biggest accomplishment is creating the cartoon *SpongeBob SquarePants* in 1999. In 2013, it won favourite cartoon of the year at the Kids' Choice Awards.

20 Write a short biography of Stephen Hillenburg. Use the information in 19. Write two more questions. Do research and find the answers. Add the information to the biography.

21 Complete the paragraphs. Use the present perfect and for or since.

I've got some amazing friends. I ¹_____ (know) my friend Anthony ²_____ we were five years old. He ³_____ (play) chess ⁴_____ 12 years and he ⁵_____ (win) many tournaments. I ⁶_____ (try) to beat him ⁷_____ many years, but I ⁸_____ (have, not) any luck! Besides being an amazing chess player, Anthony can also speak French! He wants to write and publish a book in French when he's older.

I ⁹_____ (be) friends with Stella ¹⁰_____ three years. She's an amazing musician. She ¹¹_____ (play) the piano ¹²_____ she was four years old. She also loves science. She ¹³_____ (be) a member of our school's science club ¹⁴_____ over two years. She wants to invent something one day! I'm so lucky to have such amazing friends!

22 Look at 21. Then answer the questions using complete sentences.

1 Who has won a tournament? _____
2 Who plays an instrument? _____
3 Who speaks another language? _____
4 Who wants to invent something? _____
5 Who wants to write a book? _____

23 Answer the questions. Use the present perfect continuous and since.

1 *SpongeBob SquarePants* started in 1999. How long has he been making children laugh?

_____

2 Seeds of Peace started in 1993. How long has Seeds of Peace been offering its training to teenagers?

_____

DILEMMAS

1 Look at the pictures. How do you think the people are feeling? Write the numbers.

1 angry	**2** worried	**3** upset
4 guilty	**5** happy	**6** in trouble
7 good about himself or herself		

2 Look at 1. What do you think has happened to the people? Why do they look this way? Choose one person and ✔ all possible answers. Add three of your own ideas.

The person…

- [ ] cheated in a test
- [ ] helped a friend at school
- [ ] had a fight with a friend
- [ ] _____
- [ ] heard a hurtful lie
- [ ] stopped a bully
- [ ] _____
- [ ] _____

3 Complete the dialogues. Circle the correct words.

1 Kate: Yesterday, I borrowed my mum's jacket but I lost it at the park. I don't want her to **get into trouble / be upset** with me so I'm going to tell her that someone else took it.

Sally: Why don't you check the lost property office? Maybe someone found the jacket and took it there. Then you can **feel guilty / tell the truth** and **feel good / return** the jacket to your mum.

2 Jim: My mum asked me who took the money that was on the table. I told her my little brother took it. And now he's going to **tell the truth / get into trouble** and I don't **feel guilty / feel good** about it.

Sam: You should tell your mum the truth, Jim. If you tell the truth, it'll be OK. And tell your brother that you're sorry. But who took the money?

Jim: I don't know.

4 Read the dilemma. What do you think? Complete the sentences. Use your own ideas.

You and your friend find an expensive jacket at the bus stop. There's a wallet in the pocket with an address in it. Your friend takes the jacket and returns it to the owner. The owner gives your friend a reward of £50. Your friend keeps the money and doesn't say anything to you. Then you find out the truth.

1 How do you feel?

I _____.

2 How should your friend feel?

My friend _____.

3 How do you think your friend feels?

My friend probably _____.

4 What should your friend have done?

My friend should have _____.

THINK BIG

Have you had a dilemma recently? What was it? How did you feel? What happened in the end?

_____

_____

5 Listen and read. Circle the correct answers.

GARY'S DILEMMA

Gary was walking out of school when his best friend Ryan ran up to him. "We're OK, right? If my mum calls you, you'll say it's true that I'm studying with you, right?" he whispered. Behind Ryan stood Max and a gang of boys Gary didn't want to know.

Gary nodded, trying to smile.

"Come on, Ryan, let's go, mate!" Max called.

"Just a sec!" Ryan said. He turned back to Gary. "Thanks, Gary. See you soon, OK?"

"Yeah, sure," said Gary and he turned and headed for home. How did this happen? He should have said no in the first place.

"Hey, Gary! Wait!" Gary turned and saw Pete running towards him.

"Hi, Pete," said Gary, without looking at Pete.

"What's up with you?" Pete said.

"Sorry," said Gary, "I'm just thinking about something."

"By the way," Pete said, "what's up with Ryan? What's he doing hanging out with Max and those other guys? That gang's always getting into trouble!"

"I don't know but he can do whatever he wants," shrugged Gary.

Pete grabbed Gary's shoulder. "I can't believe you said that! Ryan's our friend. If he's in trouble, we should help him."

Gary looked down, thinking, *If I tell, Ryan will think he can't trust me and I might lose him as a friend. I don't want to be in trouble with the gang, either. But if I don't tell, something terrible might happen to Ryan.* Gary had to make a decision.

1 Ryan and Gary **are / aren't** going to study together.

2 Gary **is / isn't** going to tell a lie to Ryan's mum.

3 Max and his gang **are / aren't** friends of Gary's.

4 Pete thinks he and Gary **have to / don't have** to do something to help Ryan.

6 Answer the questions. Use your own ideas.

1 Why do children join gangs? Why do you think Ryan joined the gang?

_____

2 What should Gary and Pete do?

_____

1:39

7 Listen and read. Then answer the questions.

Mum: <u>What's the matter</u>, Chris?

Chris: Nothing, Mum.

Mum: Did something happen at school today?

Chris: Well... yeah... but it's not important.

Mum: <u>Look</u>. If you don't tell me what's wrong, I can't help you. Tell me <u>what's going on</u>.

Chris: Well, a couple of boys at school are <u>being mean</u> to me.

Mum: Are they? Did they hurt you?

Chris: No, it's nothing like that. They just <u>call me names</u> sometimes.

Mum: I'm glad you told me, Chris. Let's think about what you can do.

1 What is Chris's dilemma? _____

2 What does Chris's mum want him to do? _____

3 Why doesn't Chris want to talk to his mum about his problem? _____

_____

8 Look at 7. Read the underlined expressions. Match and write the letter.

___ **1** What's the matter?

___ **2** Look.

___ **3** They're mean.

___ **4** They call me names.

___ **5** What's going on?

a They're unkind and cruel.

b What's up?

c Listen.

d What's wrong?

e They tease and insult me.

9 Answer the questions.

1 Why do you think the boys at school are being mean to Chris?

_____

2 What would you say to someone if he or she called you names?

_____

Language in Action

If he **pays attention** in class, he**'ll understand** the lesson.

If they don**'t study** for the Maths test, they **won't get** a good mark.

If you **tell** me the truth, I**'ll help** you.

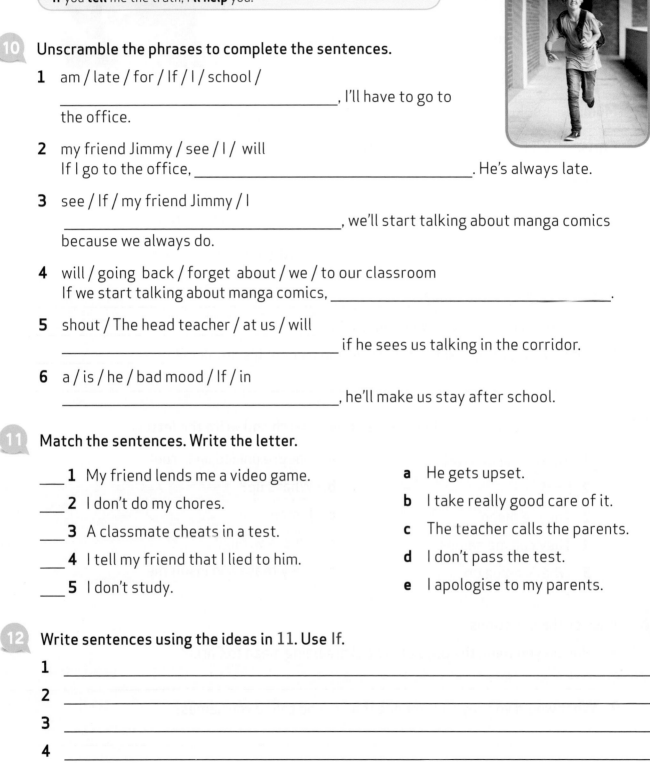

I can't be late!

10 Unscramble the phrases to complete the sentences.

1 am / late / for / If / I / school /

_____, I'll have to go to the office.

2 my friend Jimmy / see / I / will

If I go to the office, _____. He's always late.

3 see / If / my friend Jimmy / I

_____, we'll start talking about manga comics because we always do.

4 will / going back / forget about / we / to our classroom

If we start talking about manga comics, _____.

5 shout / The head teacher / at us / will

_____ if he sees us talking in the corridor.

6 a / is / he / bad mood / If / in

_____, he'll make us stay after school.

11 Match the sentences. Write the letter.

_____ **1** My friend lends me a video game.

_____ **2** I don't do my chores.

_____ **3** A classmate cheats in a test.

_____ **4** I tell my friend that I lied to him.

_____ **5** I don't study.

a He gets upset.

b I take really good care of it.

c The teacher calls the parents.

d I don't pass the test.

e I apologise to my parents.

12 Write sentences using the ideas in 11. Use If.

1 _____

2 _____

3 _____

4 _____

5 _____

> You **should tell** your parents **if** you've got a problem at school.
>
> **If** you don't want to get into trouble, you **shouldn't lie**.

13 Read the advice column. Complete the sentences with the correct form of the words in the box. Add should if necessary.

| call | find | give | say | start | stop | tell (x2) |

Ask Jenna and Jack: Smart Advice for Kids

Dear Jenna,

My friend keeps calling me names like 'stupid' and 'idiot'. She always apologises later but it makes me upset. I asked her to stop but she won't. What should I do?

Sad Samantha

Dear Sad Samantha,

This girl is NOT your friend! If this girl _____ you names again, you _____ her to apologise immediately. If she _____ no, you _____ a new friend!

Jenna

Dear Jack,

My little brother's always following me around. I feel guilty when I tell him to stop because he cries but I don't want him hanging around. My friends don't like it either. What should I do?

Guilty Gordon

Dear Guilty Gordon,

This is a difficult problem. Arrange times to play with your little brother. Then tell him that he can't follow you with your friends. If he _____ to follow you and your friends, you _____ him to stop. Tell him that you and he will play together later. If he _____ following you, you _____ him a reward. Good luck!

Jack

14 Complete the sentences with advice. Use should or shouldn't.

1 If you borrow something from a friend, _____.

2 If someone is mean to you, _____.

3 If you've got a problem at school, _____.

15 Listen and read. What does 'character' mean?

Ethics
1 Ethics is knowing what good and bad behaviour is.
2 Your **character** is all of your traits and qualities taken together, such as being friendly, honest and hard-working.
3 Treat means how you act towards others. Do you **treat** people nicely or are you mean?
4 Ethical behaviour is when you do the right thing and treat someone fairly and respectfully.

16 Read **15** again and circle the correct answers.

1 Sam is serious, clever, sometimes mean to others and impatient. These words describe ___.

   a character   **b** ethics

2 You can treat someone badly or well. *Treat* means ___.

   a the way you act with someone   **b** the way you think about someone

3 Look at the two behaviours below. The ethical behaviour is ___.

   a you see someone hurt a classmate and you don't tell because you're afraid   **b** you see someone hurt a classmate and you tell a teacher

4 When you've got a problem and you think about the right and wrong ways to act, you're thinking about ___.

   a character   **b** ethics

How do you decide what's right and what's wrong? Are there questions that you ask yourself to decide? What are they?

THINK BIG

_____

_____

_____

17 Match the proverbs to their meanings.

___ **1** "A clear conscience (mind) is a soft pillow."

___ **2** "Better to be alone than be in bad company."

___ **3** "A friend's eye is a good mirror."

a I don't need friends if they aren't good ones.

b I trust my friends to tell me the truth about myself.

c If I don't tell the truth, I won't feel good about myself (and might not be able to sleep at night).

18 Read. Who advises someone to talk to their parents?

Proverbs From Around the World

Dilemma A: ___
Nellie is a new girl at school. She's very shy so she finds it hard to make friends. A group of girls asks Nellie if she wants to be friends with them. Nellie is very happy to say yes. She feels like she's part of a group and is happy because the girls are fun to be with. But Nellie begins to notice that these girls are loud in class and don't pay much attention to the teacher. The girls notice that Nellie is good at Maths. They ask her to do their Maths homework. They say that if she doesn't, they'll tell lies about her. Nellie feels very hurt. She tells the girls that she won't be their friend any more. The girls tell lies about Nellie but Nellie doesn't care. She walks alone to school and feels good about herself.

Dilemma B: ___
Doug hasn't been doing his homework. He's stopped hanging out with his friends. He just wants to make robots and listen to music. He keeps making promises to people but he never keeps them. Today, he was supposed to help Calvin fix his bike but he didn't. Calvin stops by Doug's house. He says that Doug isn't acting like a friend. He's not being responsible. Calvin tells Doug that he should talk to his parents or to a teacher at school. Doug gets really angry and says that Calvin is stupid. Calvin leaves. Doug thinks about his behaviour and realises that Calvin is probably right. Calvin's a good friend.

Dilemma C: ___
Gloria and Zoe are Tina's best friends. They told Tina that they'd stolen some bracelets at the Craft Fair last Saturday at school. Tina's teacher thought she saw Donna near the bracelets so now everyone thinks that Donna took them. Tina doesn't know Donna well but she feels awful. Gloria and Zoe beg Tina not to tell anyone. They say they won't do it again. Tina feels very guilty. She decides to tell the truth anyway. She feels good about the decision but very sad for her friends. She hopes they understand and that they can stay friends. She knows they just made a stupid mistake.

19 Read 18 again and match the stories to their proverbs above. Write 1, 2 or 3.

20 Which proverb and story do you like best? Why?

_____

_____

Writing | Story ending

A well-written story ends in a way that seems 'right' or possible for the main character. Here are ways to help you decide what endings are 'right' or possible:

- Find information in the story about the character's traits.
- Notice how the character treats others.
- Look at the character's actions and feelings.

21 Read *Gary's Dilemma* on page 24 again. Circle the traits that describe Gary's character.

> caring   funny   honest   lazy   mean   not honest   serious   worried

22 Complete the sentences about Gary. Include one of the traits you circled in 21 and ideas from the story. Use the ideas in the box or your own ideas.

> asks his parents what he should do | says nothing and hopes that Ryan is OK
> talks to the gang members | tells a teacher about Ryan
> tells Ryan he should stop hanging around with the gang | tells Ryan's parents

I think that Gary is _____ (trait) because in the story he _____
_____ .

It's possible that he'll _____ .

I don't think that Gary will _____ .

23 Think about Gary's character. What does he do the next day? Think about these questions.

What is the first thing that he does? What happens to Gary and Ryan? Are they still friends? Why/Why not?

24 Write an ending to *Gary's Dilemma* on another piece of paper. Look at 21, 22 and 23 to help you. Begin: *The next day, Gary made a decision.*

THINK BIG

Everybody makes mistakes. When we make a mistake, what should we do? Why?

_____

_____

25 Match the expressions to the situations. Write the letters.

____ **1** tell the truth

____ **2** feel guilty

____ **3** cheat

____ **4** feel good

____ **5** get into trouble

____ **6** be upset with

a Amy looked at Suzie's test and copied the answers.

b Steve's mum is angry with him because he didn't do his homework.

c Meg feels bad because she hurt Evan's feelings.

d Mike hit Ryan in the playground and he had to go to the head teacher's office.

e Jeff said that Claire took the money. She did.

f Monica helped Robert study for his test. She's happy she could help him.

26 Write what will happen. Use will and the words in brackets.

1 Maya knows her brother cheated in a test. She wants to <u>tell her parents</u>. What will her brother do? (be / angry)

_____

2 Janet stole some money from her mum. She wants to <u>apologise to her mum</u>. What will her mum do? (say / disappointed)

_____

3 Ivy got into trouble because she was with a group of girls who called a young boy names and made him cry. She wants to <u>apologise</u>. What will he probably do? (say / OK)

_____

1 Unscramble the words. Complete the phrases.

SCHOOL ACTIVITIES

1 hand in an _____

2 do _____

3 study for a _____

4 pay _____

5 be more _____

_____ ttse _____

_____ _____ atttionen

_____ hmwokroe _____

_____ _____ ssaey

_____ cfulare _____

_____ saekp _____

_____ pbishlu _____

_____ cblmi _____

_____ boemec _____

_____ teme _____

REACHING GOALS

1 _____ a book

2 _____ a doctor

3 _____ two languages

4 _____ a world leader

5 _____ a mountain

MAKING CHOICES

1 _____ in a test

2 _____ guilty

3 be _____

4 _____ the truth

5 get into _____

_____ tspeu _____

_____ toruble

_____ fele _____

_____ eltl

_____ cetah _____

2 Find a song that makes you think about school days, goals or dilemmas. Complete the chart.

Song Title _____

Singer's or group's name _____

What language is used in the song? _____

How long have you liked this singer/group? _____

How long has this singer/group been performing? _____

What's the song about? _____

What happens in the song? _____

_____

If you can change words (lyrics) in the

song, which lyrics will you change? _____

_____

3 Draw pictures to illustrate your song. Then write the story of your song on a separate piece of paper.

DREAMS FOR THE FUTURE

1 Match the pictures to the predictions. Tick (✓) when you think the predictions may come true.

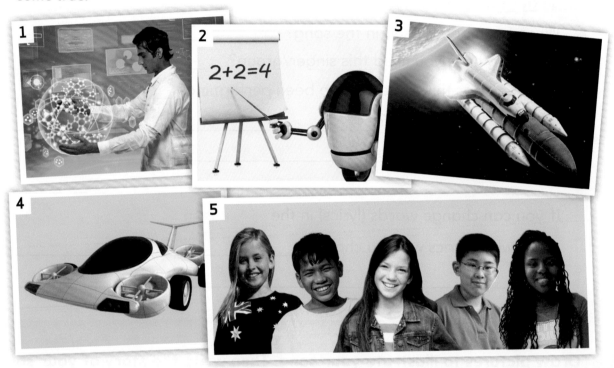

Predictions for the Future	Now	In My Lifetime	Never
___ Spaceships to other planets will be departing daily.			
___ Robots will be teaching in the classroom.			
___ People around the world will be living happily together.			
___ We'll be driving flying cars.			
___ We'll be making progress towards finding cures for many serious diseases.			

2 Look at 1. Explain one of your predictions.

_____

_____

3 Match each picture to a phrase.

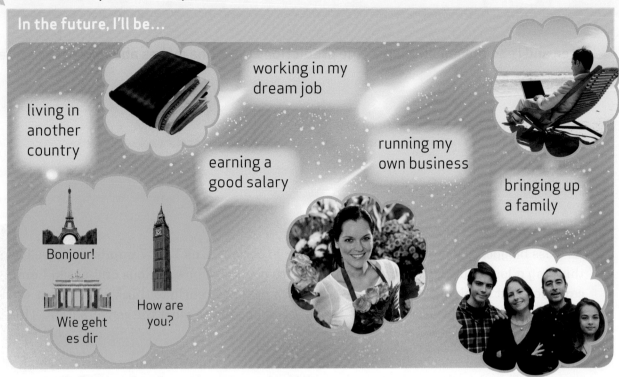

In the future, I'll be…

living in another country

working in my dream job

earning a good salary

running my own business

bringing up a family

Bonjour!

Wie geht es dir

How are you?

4 Complete the sentences with the words in 3.

1 In 20 years, I'll be _____. I really want children!

2 In 10 years, I'll be _____. I'll be a cartoonist. I've always wanted to draw cartoons. It'll be perfect!

3 In 10 years, I'll be _____ and I won't worry about money.

4 In 20 years, I'll be _____. I won't work for anyone. I'll be the boss!

5 In 10 years, I'll be _____. I'm not sure where. Maybe I'll be living in Germany.

5 Unscramble the words to complete the sentences. Are they true or false for you? Circle T for true or F for false.

1 be / my / won't / I / running / own business   T   F
In 20 years, _____.

2 a family / won't / I / bringing up / be /   T   F
In 10 years, _____.

THINK
BIG

Do you think the world will be a better or worse place thirty years from now? Why/Why not?

_____

_____

6 Listen and read the email. Then ✓ the predictions Christina makes about her classmates.

TO	classmatesall@school.org
CC	
SUBJECT	Christina's Predictions

Dear Year 7 pupils,

As class blogger, it's my job to write about our experiences as Year 7 pupils. But I've been thinking a lot about my future lately and, since you know how curious and nosey I am, I can't help but think about your futures, too. It's never too early to think about what we'll be doing in 10 or 20 years from now. I thought it'd be fun to start the conversation. This is what I predict:

I'll start with me. I know that in 10 years, I'll be running my own business in the fashion industry. That doesn't surprise you, does it?! You know how I love fashion and I also love being the boss! One thing I won't be doing is living in this city! I want to live abroad – maybe in Tokyo or Paris. Now, what about Jessie? I think he'll be working in his dream job as a cartoonist because that's all I see him doing at school. I bet he'll be making animated films. In 10 years, Stephanie will definitely be working in the music industry. She's got an amazing voice. Don't you agree? George will be taking adventurous trips abroad because he'll be a famous journalist. He's very clever and he works so hard. I hope that all of my predictions come true!

That's not all but that's all I've got time for now. If you want to reply, let me know your dreams and I'll add them to the school blog. Let's all think about our dreams and reach for the stars this year!

Your class blogger,

Christina

Predictions

☐ **1** working in his dream job   ☐ **2** living in this city

☐ **3** working in the music industry   ☐ **4** speaking foreign languages

☐ **5** earning a good salary   ☐ **6** married

☐ **7** famous   ☐ **8** taking adventurous trips

7 Make a prediction about what you'll be doing in 20 years and explain why.

I'll be _____ because _____.

8 Listen and read. Then circle the answers.

Jack: What do you think you'll be doing after you finish secondary school, Sandra?

Sandra: University, I'm sure. How about you? What will you be doing in, say, fifteen years?

Jack: I'll be working on a big film!

Sandra: A film? You think you'll be a film star?

Jack: No, not a film star. A film director. I'll be working with all the big Hollywood stars.

Sandra: Really? And how will you do that?

Jack: Well, I'm quite good at making short films on my computer already. I just need one big break! I'll be the next Sam Mendes!

Sandra: Right. I just hope you won't forget us when you're rich and famous!

Jack: Of course not! You and Mum will be walking on the red carpet with me!

Sandra: Oh, I like that idea!

1 What does Jack think he'll be doing in fifteen years?

   a He'll be acting in films.   **b** He'll be directing films.   **c** He'll be at university.

2 Young actors and singers are always looking for a big break in their career. What does "big break" mean?

   a a big rest   **b** a chance to be successful   **c** a chance to travel

3 When an actor is "on the red carpet", what is he or she invited to attend?

   a an awards ceremony   **b** university   **c** a reading of the film script

9 Read the dialogue in 8 again. Does Jack think he'll be successful? Why/Why not?

_____

_____

_____

_____

Language in Action

| What **will** you **be doing** ten years from now? | I'll definitely **be studying** at a big university. |
| Where **will** you **be living** in twenty years? | I probably **won't be living** in Europe. |

10 Match. Then answer the questions. Use the future continuous of the verbs and the word in brackets.

Hopes and Dreams in 20 years

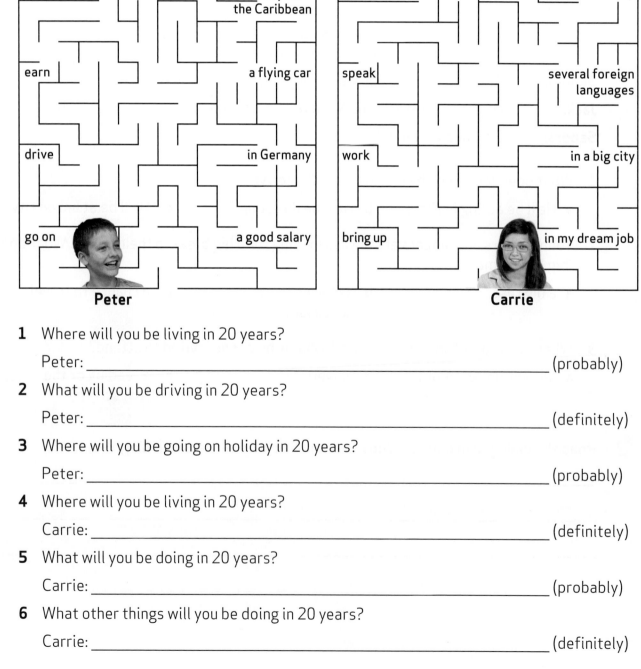

live
holidays in the Caribbean
earn
a flying car
drive
in Germany
go on
a good salary

Peter

live
a family
speak
several foreign languages
work
in a big city
bring up
in my dream job

Carrie

1 Where will you be living in 20 years?

Peter: _____ (probably)

2 What will you be driving in 20 years?

Peter: _____ (definitely)

3 Where will you be going on holiday in 20 years?

Peter: _____ (probably)

4 Where will you be living in 20 years?

Carrie: _____ (definitely)

5 What will you be doing in 20 years?

Carrie: _____ (probably)

6 What other things will you be doing in 20 years?

Carrie: _____ (definitely)

Will you **be running** a business?	No, definitely not. I definitely **won't**…
	Yes, definitely. I definitely **will**…
	Probably not. I probably **won't**…
	Yes, probably. I probably **will**…

11 **Answer the questions. Use the information in 10.**

1 Will Carrie be working in her dream job in 20 years?

_____

2 Will Peter be living in Germany in 20 years?

_____

3 Will Carrie be living in a small city in 20 years?

_____

4 Will Peter be going on holiday in Asia?

_____

5 Will Carrie be bringing up a family in 20 years?

_____

6 Will Peter be driving a flying car in 20 years?

_____

12 **Answer the questions about your future life at university with No, definitely not, Yes, definitely or Probably not.**

1 Will you be seeing your family a lot when you go to university?

_____

2 Will you be studying a foreign language at university?

_____

3 Will you be studying harder than you do now?

_____

13 **Choose a friend. Write a question about your friend's future at university. Ask your friend the question. Then write the answer No, definitely not, Yes, definitely or Probably not.**

Q: _____

A: _____

2:09

14 Listen and read. What will doctors use nanobots for in the future?

Two Trends in Medicine

There are two important trends in the future of medicine. One is nanotechnology. The word *nano* means billionth. That's really tiny! Scientists who are working in nanotechnology are studying particles that are so small that they are invisible to the human eye! In fact, they have to measure these particles with a new unit of measurement, called the nanometre. Do you see the word 'metre' in nanometre? You know how long a metre is, don't you? For example, a cricket bat is a little shorter than one metre in length. Can you imagine something that is only 1/1,000,000,000 of a cricket bat? One example of this is the nanobot. These microscopic robots are made of the same material that we are made of: DNA. In the future, scientists will be using nanobots to treat diseases and illnesses. For example, when you become ill in the future, doctors will put a nanobot into your body. The robot will find the cause of your illness and give you the correct medicine to help it heal. Wouldn't that be great? Think about it: When you become ill, your insides will be like a video game: robots will be searching for 'the baddies' and destroying them!

The second trend is in virtual medicine. Thirty years from now, when you've got a fever and feel ill, you won't have to leave the house to go to a doctor. You'll be using wireless technology to diagnose and treat your illness in your own home. In this futuristic scenario, you'll take 3D pictures of your body using an object like a TV remote control. You'll upload these images to a website. The doctor will download the images, review them and upload medicine for you to download. If the doctor wants to talk to you, he or she will talk to you through a video call – or maybe he or she will 'visit' you virtually using 3D technology. The doctor will look like he or she is in your house but it will just be a 3D image. Wouldn't that be amazing?

15 Think about the size of things around you. The head of a pin is 2,000,000 (two million) nanometres wide. What's the size of these objects in nanometres? Guess and circle.

1 An ant is about ___ nanometres wide.

  a 5,000 **b** 50,000 **c** 5,000,000

2 A human hair is about ___ nanometres wide.

  a 12,000 **b** 120,000 **c** 1,200,000

3 A man who is two metres tall is ___ nanometres tall.

  a 2 million **b** 2 billion **c** 2 trillion

16 Read. What did the children want computers to look and act like?

Young Inventors

What will your future look like? It depends on the inventions that inventors are dreaming up today, doesn't it? And who are those inventors? You might think that inventors are old people who have worked for many years on their ideas. That may have been what inventors looked like years ago but in this technological age, that view of inventors is quickly disappearing.

Researchers today think the ideas for inventions will come from children. They recently interviewed children, aged 12 and under, from all around the world and asked them what they thought computers would be like in the future. They were amazed by how many wonderful and inventive ideas the children talked about. These children were very comfortable with technology and they wanted to see computers do more and more for them. In fact, the children wanted computers to look and act human. They didn't think it would be strange to have a computer as a friend! They had some differences of opinion about what exactly they wanted computers to do. Some children said they wanted computers that would play with them and help them with homework. Other children wanted to use computers to learn new skills and do things more easily like speaking a foreign language. Others wanted to use computers to create things like video games and virtual-reality places.

Everyone thought it'd be great if they could mix online and real-life experiences. For example, they wanted to be able to see things online – like a sandwich – and make it into a real sandwich using a machine like a printer. Sounds cool, doesn't it?

What do you think about these ideas? Do you agree that children like you will be creating new inventions for the future? Maybe you've got an idea for an invention. If you have, draw it, write about it and tell someone! You might be the next Steve Jobs!

17 Read 16 again and answer the questions.

1 Do you think children are better than adults at thinking up new ideas with computers? Why/Why not?

_____

_____

2 The children had different ideas about computers. What do you want computers to do?

_____

_____

THINK BIG

The children liked the idea of seeing something on the computer – like a sandwich – and making it real using a machine. What would you like to make real?

_____

_____

When you write an email, you need to think about who you're writing to. If you're writing to a teacher or other adult, you'll write a formal email. If you're writing to a friend, you'll write an informal email. Here are some ways these two kinds of emails are different.

	Formal Email	Informal Email
1 Subject	1 Be clear and specific. *This week's essay*	1 Write something simple. *Tonight* or *Hi*
2 Greeting	2 Use Ms / Mr / Mrs. *Mrs Smith,*	2 Write *Hi Tony,* or *Hey Tony,*
3 Body	3 Write your message in full sentences, check your spelling and be polite. *I missed school yesterday because I was ill. Can you tell me what the homework is, please?*	3 u can use short words coz u wanna write quickly to ur bff.
4 Closing	4 Write *Yours sincerely* or *Best wishes* and your name below.	4 Write your name.

18 Read each sentence. Write formal if it belongs in a formal email or informal if it belongs in an informal email. Add commas where necessary.

1 _____ Hey Tami,

2 _____ I am having trouble deciding what to do for my Science project. Could you help me think of some ideas?

3 _____ c u later bff!

4 _____ Dear Mr Taylor,

5 _____ Yours sincerely, Steve

19 Write formal and informal emails on a separate piece of paper. In the informal email, use abbreviations from the Tips box.

Tips

Texting Abbreviations

b4 = before

bff = best friends forever

c = see

coz = because

gonna = going to

TTYL = talk to you later

u = you

wanna = want to

THINK BIG

Why do we use different language, formal and informal, when talking to different people?

_____

_____

Review

20 Complete the sentences. Use the future continuous of the verbs in brackets.

Chris and his sister, Ann, have got big plans for the future. Chris ¹_____ probably _____ (go) to university in ten years. Once he graduates, he ²_____ (work) as a businessman with his dad. He definitely ³_____ (not live) in another country because he wants to stay close to his family in Leeds.

Ann ⁴_____ probably _____ (study) biology at university. She's always wanted to be a scientist. In 20 years, she ⁵_____ definitely _____ (earn) a good salary. She probably ⁶_____ (not live) in the UK because she's always wanted to live in a foreign country.

Both Chris and Ann ⁷_____ (bring up) big families. They both want to have lots of children.

21 Choose a member of your own family. Complete the sentences about that family member's future using the future continuous. Use will or won't and the words from the box or your own words.

dream job	earning a good salary	famous
going on adventurous holidays	married	running his or her own business

1 My family member's name is _____ .
2 This person _____ in 10 years.
3 This person _____ in 20 years.

22 Answer the questions. Use Yes, definitely, Yes, probably, No, probably not or No, definitely not.

1 In your lifetime, do you think you'll be working with intelligent beings from outer space?

_____

2 Do you think people will be living on other planets in the next century?

_____

IF I COULD FLY...

unit 5

1 Which super powers have these characters got? Match the characters to their super power. Write the numbers.

___ able to climb tall buildings

___ runs faster than the wind

___ saves the world from 'bad guys'

___ has got superhuman strength

___ disappears with the snap of a finger

___ travels through time and space

2 Look at 1 and answer the questions.

1 Which super power would make your life better?

_____

2 How would the super power improve your life?

_____

3 Who are your favourite superheroes? What powers have they got?

_____

3 Match the beginning of the phrases to their endings. Then match the phrases to the pictures. Write the numbers under the pictures.

Now you see me!

It's easy!

Now you don't!

A ___   B ___   C ___   D ___

___ **1** run at   **a** invisible
___ **2** travel   **b** superhuman strength
___ **3** have   **c** lightning speed
___ **4** become   **d** through time

4 Complete the sentences with the phrases in 3.

1 I want to meet people who lived long ago. If I could have a super power, I would _____.

2 I want to move around without people being able to see me. If I could have a super power, I would _____.

3 I want to be able to get anywhere in a few seconds! If I could have a super power, I would _____.

4 I want to be really strong so that I can pick up anything I want! If I could have a super power, I would _____.

5 Complete the sentences. If you had these superpowers, what would you do?

1 If I could have superhuman strength, I would _____.

2 If I could read minds, I would _____.

3 If I could travel through time, I would _____.

Which super powers could help the police? How?

THINK
BIG
_____
_____
_____

6 Listen and read. Then circle T for true or F for false.

1	Bulldog and Power Paws know each other.	T	F
2	Bulldog is happy to see Power Paws.	T	F
3	Bulldog isn't scared of Power Paws.	T	F
4	Bulldog knows that Power Paws is going to make him small.	T	F
5	Power Paws has got special powers.	T	F

7 Answer the questions.

1 What's Bulldog doing to Duck?

_____

2 Why is Power Paws going to make Bulldog small?

_____

3 Do you think Duck will take good care of Bulldog?

_____

2:20

8 Listen and read. Then circle the correct answers.

Girl: Dad, do you think we'll ever be able to travel through time?

Dad: Wow, <u>that's a hard one</u>. A lot's possible today but I really don't see how time travel would be. Why do you ask?

Girl: I was just wondering. Imagine how much fun it would be if we could! If you could <u>go back in time</u>, where would you go?

Dad: Hmm. <u>Let me think</u>… Maybe I'd go back to see my great-grandparents who lived in London. My great-grandfather was a shoemaker there – have I ever told you that? I'm told he was <u>quite a character</u>. I'd love to talk to him. What would you do?

Girl: Me? Oh, I already know – that's easy. If I could travel through time, I'd go back to last night and revise more. I don't feel ready for my Maths test this afternoon!

1 The dad thinks the girl's question is ___ to answer.

  a easy   **b** not easy

2 The girl ___ travel back in time.

  a wants to   **b** doesn't want to

3 The girl ___ stories about her great-grandfather.

  a has heard   **b** hasn't heard

4 The girl ___ hard for her Maths test.

  a studied   **b** didn't study

9 Match the phrases to their meanings.

___ **1** That's a hard one.

___ **2** go back in time

___ **3** quite a character

___ **4** Let me think.

  a It means 'to travel to a time in the past'.

  b It means 'a funny, interesting, unique person' that people like.

  c It means 'I need a little time to think about my answer'.

  d It means 'That's a difficult question'. You say this when the question isn't easy to answer.

10 Complete the sentence. Use a phrase from 9.

The teacher asks you, "Who's your favourite superhero?" You need to think about your answer so you say _____ .

Language in Action

if clause	result clause
If I **were** you,	I**'d choose** something else.
If he **made** his bed every day,	his mum **would be** happy.
If she **could have** one super power,	she**'d breathe** underwater.

11 Complete the sentences with the words given.

1 (would, study, were) If I _____ you,
   I _____ harder. You would get better marks.

2 (could, would, fly, visit) If she _____ ,
   she _____ her aunt and uncle in Scotland all the time.

3 (could, would, run, win) If the athletics team _____ at
   lightning speed, it _____ all its competitions.

4 (would, be, did) If all the pupils _____ their homework all
   the time, the teacher _____ happy.

5 (could, would, know, read) If I _____ my teacher's mind,
   I _____ the answers to all her questions.

12 Read. Complete the speech bubbles with the words given. Use could and would.

I can't sing well. But if I _____
(sing) well, I _____ (join) a band.

My friends and I can't travel back in time. If
we _____ (travel) back in time,
we _____ (meet) our favourite
heroes in history.

My older brother can't drive yet. If he
_____ (drive), he
_____ (take) me and my
friends to the cinema.

My friend can't be quiet in class. If she
_____ (be) quiet, our
teacher _____ (be) happier.

13 Complete the sentences about yourself.

1 If I could meet a famous person, I _____ .

2 _____ , I would be very happy.

| If you **didn't have to go** to school, what **would** you **do** every day? | If I **didn't have to go** to school, I **would stay** home and **listen** to music all day. |
| If you **could go** anywhere, where **would** you **go**? | If I **could go** anywhere, I**'d go** to Paris. |

14 Complete the questions. Unscramble the words.

(you / would / go / where)

1 If you could visit any country you wanted to, _____?

(would / which language / you / learn)

2 If you could learn another language (not English), _____?

(you / be / would / which animal)

3 If you could be any animal, _____?

(be / who / you / would)

4 If you could be any superhero, _____?

(would / play / which instrument / you)

5 If you could play any instrument, _____?

15 Match the questions in 14 to the answers below. Write the numbers. Then circle T for true or F for false.

___ **1** I would be a wolf because wolves are really clever animals.   T   F

___ **2** I would visit Italy to see the works of art.   T   F

___ **3** I would learn Chinese.   T   F

___ **4** I would be Spider-Man because I think it would be fun to climb walls.   T   F

___ **5** I would play the piano.   T   F

16 Ask a friend or family member the questions in 14. Write his or her answers.

1 _____

2 _____

3 _____

4 _____

5 _____

17 Listen and read. Have researchers discovered how to give us perfect memory?

Super Power or Invention?

Some researchers have developed products that seem to give us super power-like abilities. One of these inventions is the super sticky adhesive that they created by studying geckos and their sticky feet. Another invention is the ability to tell a computer what to do with our minds. A third invention is our ability to visualise a computer anywhere we want one – even on our hands. Let's think about what our lives might be like if we had these products today.

In the morning, you wake up. Your bed is stuck on the wall so you climb down a ladder to get to the floor. There is space under your bed now to hang out with friends so you like that. After breakfast, you put on your super sticky shoes and hand pads. On your way to school, you climb up a wall to your friend Timmy's bedroom window. He sees you. You both climb down the wall and start walking to school.

"Oh, no!" you suddenly say, "I've forgotten my homework!" You think, *Mum, please send my Maths homework to school.* Your mum gets the message on her smartphone and texts back, "OK." You think, *Thanks, Mum!* Your mind is connected to your computer at home so you can send messages to it or to your parents' smartphones. Then your friend says, "I wonder what the reviews are for the new superhero film?" He draws a box on your backpack and a computer appears. He goes to a film review website and reads the latest reviews to you as you walk.

At school, you climb up the wall and hang your jacket on a hook. Your teacher gives you a quiz and tells you, "Don't draw computers anywhere. If you've studied, you'll know every answer." You didn't study much so you're thinking, *If I could see the book in my mind, I could look up the answers.* Researchers haven't worked out how to give you perfect memory – but they're probably working on it.

18 Read 17 again and answer the questions.

1 Where did the idea of a sticky adhesive come from?

_____

2 'To develop something' means it took a long time to make something work well. Which invention do you think would take the longest to create? Why?

_____

3 Do you think it would be fun to walk up walls? If so, why?

_____

THINK BIG Pretend that you can draw computers anywhere and use them. Where would you use them? What would you do?

_____

19 Read. Where is Darna from?

Superheros from Around the World

Superheroes from around the world have got unique abilities to help them protect people and destroy evil.

Cat Girl Nuku Nuku is from Japan. She's a university student but when something terrible happens, she becomes a superhero! She can react quickly when something bad happens, just like a cat. She can smell, see and hear very well because she's got the senses of a cat. She's also got superhuman strength.

Meteroix is from Mexico. He's at university, too and his everyday name is Aldo. He's also got superhuman strength and can throw bolts of lightning. When he has to protect himself, he covers himself with blue armour by swallowing a meteorite.

Darna is from the Philippines. Her everyday name is Narda and she's a student as well. Darna can fly and has got superhuman strength and speed. She can't be destroyed by weapons that humans make. She can change back and forth between her two identities by swallowing a stone and shouting the name of her other identity.

Superheroes are fun to read about but do you sometimes wish that they were real? If these superheroes were real, they would have lots of things to do every day!

20 Read 19 again and write the names of the superheroes.

1 Human weapons cannot destroy this superhero. _____

2 Bolts of lightning are weapons of this superhero. _____

3 This superhero acts like a cat. _____

21 Read. Which superhero can help? Why?

1 Some bank robbers are coming out of a bank. They've got a very big weapon. They're running away!

_____

2 An evil person from space wants to steal all the gold and diamonds in the world. It's hard to find her because she's very tiny and can hide very easily. She loves biscuits and she's always got some in her pockets.

_____

3 Some bad guys have got thousands of fighters helping them. The bad guys want to destroy the government. The bad guys are attacking now!

_____

When you write a description of a character, describe everything about that character:

1 name(s)
2 appearance
3 occupation
4 super powers
5 country of origin
6 family
7 time period that he or she lives in: now, the future, the past
8 mission

22 Read the sentences and match them to the information in the box. Write the numbers. Be careful! What information is missing? Write the numbers.

___ Her everyday name is Diana but her superhero name is Wonder Woman.

___ She's got superhuman strength and she's an excellent fighter. She's got a rope that makes people tell the truth and an invisible jet.

___ She's from a place near Greece in ancient times.

___ She's got a lot of sisters.

Missing information: Numbers ___ ___ ___ ___

23 Read the missing information from 22 below. Number it according to the information in the writing box.

___ lived in the past and lives in the present, too	___ make villains honest
___ in many stories she's an officer in the army	___ is tall / has got long dark hair

24 Write a description of Wonder Woman. Use the information in 22 and 23.

_____

_____

_____

_____

_____

_____

25 Match the phrases to make sentences. Write the letters.

___ **1** If I could read people's minds,

___ **2** If I could run at lightning speed,

___ **3** If I could travel through time,

___ **4** If I could fly,

a I'd be faster than a train.

b I'd know what they were thinking.

c I'd go back and play with my grandad when he was young.

d I'd take my brothers and sisters for rides in the sky with me.

26 Complete the sentences with your own ideas.

1 If _____ , I'd know why you're angry with me.

2 If _____ , I'd move your house closer to mine. Then I could see you more often.

3 If I could invent something to help other people, _____ .

4 If I _____ , my family would be very happy.

27 Read. Circle the correct answers.

1 If people ___ wings, they wouldn't drive cars.

   a have   **b** had

2 If she had enough money, she ___ those silver earrings.

   a 'd buy   **b** buys

3 You're really clever. If I ___ you, I'd try out for a TV quiz show.

   a were   **b** be

4 If my older brother went to bed earlier, he ___ so tired every morning.

   a 's not going to be   **b** wouldn't be

28 Answer the questions with your own ideas.

1 If you found £20, what would you do with the money?

_____

2 If you wrote a book, what would you write about?

_____

3 If you owned a flying car, where would you go and why?

_____

unit 6

THE COOLEST SCHOOL SUBJECTS

1 Which school subjects do the pictures show? Write the numbers.

___ Geography

___ History of Art

___ Science

___ Music

___ Literature

___ World History

___ P.E.

___ Maths

2 If you could choose three subjects to add to your school timetable, what would they be? Tick (✔) or add your own ideas.

☐ Computer Science

☐ Chinese

☐ Orchestra

☐ Theatre

☐ _____

☐ Government

☐ Chemistry

☐ Tennis

☐ Ecosystems and Ecology

☐ _____

3 Unscramble the words. Use the words to complete the sentences.

1 M Y C R O E A C D _____

The word _____ comes from a Greek word that means 'power of the people'. One of the first Western examples of this form of government was in Athens, in the 5th century BC.

2 M A M L A M _____

The cheetah is the fastest _____ in the world. It can run about 100 metres in six seconds!

3 P T N A L _____

The bladderwort is the deadliest meat-eating _____. It can kill an insect in less than a millisecond.

4 G I Y R H W A L T P S _____

Shakespeare is one of the most famous _____ in English literature. He wrote approximately 40 plays in his lifetime, including comedies, tragedies and historical plays.

5 P E R M I B E U R N M _____ _____

The number 8 can be divided by 1 and 8 but it can also be divided by 2 and 4. As a result, it is not a _____ _____.

4 Match these sentences to the subjects. Write the letters.

___**1** I want to learn more about myths and legends.

___**2** I love reading about democracies all over the world.

___**3** We've got a grammar test today.

___**4** In today's lesson, we learnt that blue whales are the largest mammals in the world!

___**5** We're painting a mural on the wall today.

___**6** I love playing football!

a P.E.

b English

c Literature

d Art

e Social Science

f Science (Biology)

THINK BIG

Is what you learn inside the classroom and what you learn outside the classroom equally important? Why/Why not?

_____

_____

2:30
5 Listen and read. Then answer the questions.

The Story of Daedalus and Icarus

Once upon a time, on the island of Crete, there was a man named Daedalus and his young son Icarus. They lived in the palace of King Minos. Daedalus was the cleverest man in the palace. He was also one of the greatest inventors and architects of that time. He invented many things for the king, including an enormous type of maze called The Labyrinth. King Minos didn't want Daedalus to share the secrets of The Labyrinth with anyone so he put Daedalus and Icarus in prison. Daedalus was very unhappy. He had only one wish. He wanted to be free.

One day, Daedalus was watching the birds fly. He admired their beautiful, strong wings. Watching the birds gave him an idea. If he created wings for Icarus and himself, they could fly away and be free! So Daedalus created wings of feathers and wax and they put them on. Daedalus told Icarus, "Be careful! Don't fly too close to the water or you might fall into it! Don't fly too close to the sun or the wax will melt and you'll fall!" Icarus said that he would obey his father but when they started flying, Icarus became extremely excited. He flew in circles and went higher and higher. He loved the feeling of freedom and flying. His father called out to him, "Come back here! Don't go too close to the sun!" Icarus wanted to listen but the feeling of freedom was the best feeling in the world so he kept flying higher. The sun became hotter and hotter and began to melt the wax. Icarus started to fly lower but it was too late. Icarus's wings fell off and he fell into the sea and was lost.

1 Why did King Minos put Daedalus and Icarus in prison?

_____

2 Why did Daedalus want to escape?

_____

3 Why did Icarus fly higher and higher?

_____

4 What can we learn from this story?

_____

5 The Icarian Sea was named after Icarus. Do you know any other places named after famous myths and legends? Write the names.

_____

2:33

6 Listen and read. Then circle the correct answers.

Julie: I haven't revised for the Maths test yet, have you?

Leo: Not yet. Hey, <u>let's make a study group</u>!

Julie: That's the cleverest idea you've had in a long time!

Leo: Ha! Ha! Very funny.

Cathy: Brilliant idea! The only thing I remember about prime numbers is that they're larger than 1.

Julie: <u>Speaking of</u> prime numbers, do you know the most amazing thing about the numbers 3-7-9-0-0-9? Type them on a calculator and read them upside down. They spell GOOGLE.

Leo: <u>Seriously</u>? <u>Let me see</u>… You're right! That's the coolest thing ever!

379 009

1 Why are Julie, Leo and Cathy going to get together?

  a They're going to have fun. **b** They're going to revise for the Maths test.

2 Does Cathy understand what prime numbers are?

  a Yes. **b** No.

3 Why is 379009 an amazing number?

  a It spells the word 'GOOGLE' in numbers. **b** It's the largest prime number.

7 Look at 6. Read the underlined expressions. How can you say them in other words? Match the expressions to the sentences. Write the letters.

___ **1** Let's make a study group.

___ **2** Speaking of…

___ **3** Let me see.

___ **4** Seriously?

a By the way, that reminds me of something.

b Really? I'm surprised.

c Why don't we study together?

d I want to try.

2:34

8 Complete the dialogues with the expressions in 7. Then listen and check your answers.

A: I was just chosen to be on a TV quiz programme.

B: ¹_____? Congratulations!

01134

A: Yeah, they asked me what happens when you turn 01134 upside down. I said it spells 'hello'.

B: ²_____. Wow! You're right!

A: ³_____ numbers, ⁴_____ for the Maths test tomorrow.

B: Good idea!

Language in Action

China's got **more** speakers of English **than** the USA.

I've got **fewer** school subjects **than** my brother.

Teachers in Finland give **less** homework **than** teachers in the UK.

9 Complete these facts about countries. Circle more, fewer or less.

1 People in Germany spend 18 hours a week watching TV. People in the UK spend 28 hours. People in the UK spend **less / more** time watching TV than people in Germany.

2 According to the World Atlas, Europe has got 47 countries and Asia has got 44 countries. There are **more / less** countries in Europe than in Asia.

3 In Spain, there are approximately 19,000 males and 20,000 females. There are **less / fewer** males than females.

4 In Africa, people speak more than 2,000 languages. In North and South America, people speak almost 1,000 languages. People in Africa speak **more / less** languages than people in North and South America.

5 In the UK, the parrot is a **more / less** popular pet than a cat. People like cats better than parrots.

6 In India, 946 films are made per year. In the USA, 611 films are made per year. The USA makes **more / fewer** films per year than India.

10 Answer the questions. Write complete sentences.

1 Do you watch more or fewer hours of TV a week than people in the UK?

_____

2 In your country, do you think a rabbit is a more or less popular pet than a cat?

_____

3 Do you think your country makes fewer or more films per year than the USA?

_____

4 Do you think your country has got more or fewer people than the UK?

_____

5 In your class, are there more females or males?

_____

> The Amazon rainforest has got **the most** species of plants and animals on Earth.
>
> Germany and Switzerland have got **the fewest** pet dogs per capita.
>
> Which country has got **the least** amount of air pollution?

11 **Draw lines to connect the sentence parts.**

1 A tree in Nevada, USA, is 4,800 years old. It's	the least	tourists of any city in Europe.
2 London has about 15 million tourists each year. It has	the longest	mammal in the world.
3 The kakapo parrot weighs 3.5 kilograms. It's	the oldest	amount of rain a year of all deserts.
4 It rarely rains in the Atacama Desert in Chile. It's got	the lightest	parrot in the world.
5 Siberia has got a very long railway. It's got	the heaviest	railway in the world.
6 The bumblebee bat only weighs two grams. It's	the most	tree alive.

12 **Read the answers. Write the questions.**

1 _____

The armadillo is one of the most endangered species in the Americas.

2 _____

The piranha has got the sharpest teeth of all fish.

3 _____

The white millipede has got the most legs of any animal. It's got a total of 750 wiggling legs!

4 _____

The land mammal with the fewest teeth is the narwhal. It's only got two, large teeth.

2:36

13 Write the words in the correct category. Then listen and check your answers.

| algae | carnivore | herbivore |
| nectar | nutrient | protein |

Words that describe animals	Words that describe plants	Words that describe food

14 Read. How tall can a pitcher plant grow?

How to Take Care of a Pitcher Plant

   If your parents won't allow pets in your home, you could try growing a pitcher plant. It could be your perfect 'pet plant'. You can take care of it and feed it just like a pet. But be careful. At mealtimes, these plants get very hungry! So hungry they could eat a rat! Yes, this plant is the largest meat-eating plant in the world. In fact, pitcher plants can grow up to one metre tall!

   Pitcher plants need lots of nutrients and protein. To be a good pitcher plant owner, you'll have to make sure that your plant gets lots of sunlight and water. These are important to keep your little carnivore happy and healthy. Water's especially important. It makes the top of the plant slippery so that insects can slip into the nectar. The sweet-smelling sticky nectar helps the plant digest the food.

   Check your plant to make sure it's catching enough insects. Some days you'll have to feed it an extra insect or two if it looks hungry. Your pitcher plant will have the healthiest and happiest pet plant life of all if you love it and take good care of it.

15 Read 14 again and answer the questions.

1 What's unusual about the pitcher plant?

_____

2 How can you keep a pitcher plant healthy?

_____

THINK BIG Would you like to own a pitcher plant? Would it make a good pet?

_____

2:38
16 Read the words in the box and look at the chart. Then listen and write the words in the correct place.

Arabic zero (0)	calendar	chocolate	democracy	herbal remedies
myths	number system	Olympic Games	terraced farming	

The Greeks
- Literature _____
- Sports _____
- Politics _____

The Maya
- Astronomy _____
- Maths _____

The Aztecs
- Maths _____
- Food _____

The Inca
- Social Science _____
- Medicine _____

17 Which ancient civilisation should you thank for things you've got today? Read and write The Greeks, The Aztecs, The Maya or The Inca.

1 Your favourite football team can compete to be the best in the world at the Olympic Games.

_____

2 The people in Thailand and Vietnam grow rice and other crops on hills.

_____

3 When you get hungry and want something sweet, you eat a chocolate bar.

_____

4 When you get ill, your mum or doctor might give you herbal remedies to make you feel better.

_____

5 When you get bored, you can read incredible stories about heroes, gods and goddesses.

_____

18 Think and write about one more thing that you should thank an ancient civilisation for.

_____

_____

A play tells a story. Both a play and a story have got…

- Characters
- Important events
- An order of events

But a play is a special kind of story. It tells the story through dialogues and actors speaking those dialogues. The dialogues show what the people want, what they're thinking and what's happening or has happened. The dialogue is the only thing that tells us about the characters and events.

19 Read the story of Daedalus and Icarus in 5 again. Answer the questions.

1 How many characters are there in the story?

_____

2 What are the names of the characters?

_____

3 How would you describe each of the characters?

_____

_____

4 There are three events mentioned in the story.

What happened first? _____

What happened second? _____

What happened in the end? _____

5 What do these characters say, think or wish in the story?

King Minos: _____

_____

Daedalus: _____

_____

Icarus: _____

_____

20 On a separate piece of paper, rewrite one of the events as a play. Tell the story of the event as a dialogue between two of the characters. Use your notes in 19.

21 **Read and write.**

1 Write an example of a prime number: _____

2 Write the name of a famous artist: _____

3 Write the name of a sport that is played in the Olympic Games: _____

4 Write the name of a famous playwright: _____

22 **Read and complete the sentences with more or fewer.**

1 A spider has got eight legs. An ant has got six legs.

The spider has got _____ than an ant.

2 I've got two pets. My friend Alex has got three pets.

I've got _____ than Alex.

3 London has got about 8 million people. Birmingham has got almost 1 million people.

London has got _____ than Birmingham.

4 My pitcher plant eats four insects a day. Your pitcher plant eats six insects a day.

My pitcher plant eats _____ than yours.

23 **Complete the sentences. Use the least, the fewest or the most and the underlined words.**

1 Children in Finland don't do much <u>homework</u>.

They _____ of any European country.

2 France has got a lot of <u>pet owners</u>.

It _____ of any European country.

3 Canada has got a small number of <u>mammals</u>.

It _____ of any country in the world.

4 Approximately 32 percent of families in the USA own <u>dogs</u>. That's more than any other country.

It _____ of any country in the world.

5 <u>People</u> don't live permanently in Antarctica.

It _____ of any other continent.

THINK BIG

1 Look at Units 4, 5 and 6. Choose words from the units. Write them in the charts.

DREAMS FOR THE FUTURE

_____

_____

_____

_____

SUPER POWERS

_____

_____

_____

_____

SCHOOL INTERESTS

_____

_____

_____

_____

2 Make a list of your superheroes – real or imaginary.

3 Look at **2**. Choose one superhero and make some notes about your choice.

His/Her Dreams

_____

_____

_____

His/Her Powers

_____

_____

_____

His/Her Interests

_____

_____

_____

4 Look at **1**, **2** and **3**. Write a song about your superhero. Use some of these sentences in your song. Add your own sentences.

I'll save my best numbers for you.

If I could fly like Superman…

Pow! Bam! Slam! Kaboom!

Superhero, here I am.

I'll be living on the moon.

I've got my super power.

I'll be travelling through time soon.

unit 7 MYSTERIES

1 Match the pictures to the explanations of these unsolved mysteries. What do you think? Are these explanations possible? Circle Possible or Not Possible.

	Possible	Not Possible
___ Overnight, the wind creates unusual circles in farmer's fields.	**Possible**	**Not Possible**
___ Giant pre-historic ape-like men still live in the Himalayas of Asia.	**Possible**	**Not Possible**
___ Large, heavy rocks weighing up to 300 kilos move from place to place by themselves.	**Possible**	**Not Possible**
___ The 246-page, 15th-century book of drawings and strange letters was written as a hoax to fool people and it doesn't really mean anything.	**Possible**	**Not Possible**
___ Aliens from outer space created perfectly round sculptures in Costa Rica.	**Possible**	**Not Possible**

2 Complete the dialogues. Then listen and check your answers.

3:03

| explanation | Great Pyramids | northern lights | proof |
| scientific | theories | unsolved | |

A: Have you ever heard of the ¹_____?

B: Yes, I think so. They're those bright colourful lights in the night sky. They're caused by light reflecting off the ice caps in the Arctic.

A: No, that was just a theory. Now there's ²_____

³_____ . Gases in the air cause these nighttime fireworks.

A: The ⁴_____ in Egypt are incredible, aren't they?

B: They certainly are. Has anyone got an ⁵_____ of how they were built?

A: Well, some scientists have got ⁶_____ about it but the mystery is still ⁷_____ .

3 Read the sentences about the places in 2. Circle T for true or F for false. Correct the false sentences.

1 The Great Pyramids are an unsolved mystery but scientists have got some theories about them.   T   F

_____

2 There is scientific proof about how the Great Pyramids were built.   T   F

_____   T   F

3 The northern lights appear in the night sky over Egypt.   T   F

_____   T   F

THINK BIG

Do you think that most mysteries can be explained by science? Why/Why not?

_____

_____

3:05

Listen and read. Then answer the questions.

The Voynich Manuscript

The Voynich manuscript, written in the 15th century in Western Europe, is beautiful to look at. The pages of this 'book' are full of colourful, lovely drawings of plants and astronomical objects, like suns and moons. The handwriting that surrounds the drawings appears to describe herbal remedies from plants. You can imagine that the author was a doctor or a scientist. But if you look more closely, you'll notice two very strange things: The words aren't in any known language and the plants don't exist. That's incredible, isn't it?

Scientists have studied the Voynich manuscript for years and have tried to understand the meaning of the words and the strange drawings. The words do follow some 'rules' of a language or even two languages but scientists still cannot work out what the language is. And they don't know where the author learnt about the strange plants. An early theory was that the writer used an artificial language. Another theory was that the whole thing was a hoax. But why would someone spend so much time on a manuscript and work so hard if it was just a prank?

Today, a group of scientists around the world are working together to create a machine that will help them finally crack the code. What do you think? Will a computer be able to help them understand the information that the 15th-century writer so beautifully and carefully put into this manuscript?

COMMENTS (2)

Savvy Sam

This is fascinating! What theories have scientists got about the plants? Could the plants be extinct species? They're amazing!

Georgina

I agree with Savvy Sam. The plants are amazing. I wonder if the plants look different because they're ancient? Plants could change over time, couldn't they? I hope scientists crack the code soon. Maybe the manuscript contains the cure for today's diseases. You never know!

1 How old is the Voynich manuscript?

_____

2 What's strange about the Voynich manuscript?

_____

3:08

5 Listen and read. Then circle T for true or F for false.

Tony: I got you <u>hooked on</u> Kryptos, didn't I?

Gerald: You really did! I found lots of <u>cool stuff</u> about Kryptos online. Did you know that the creator of the codes has given more clues recently?

Tony: Seriously? What are the new clues?

Gerald: He gave six letters out of the 97 in the last phrase.

Tony: I bet the decoders got excited, didn't they?

Gerald: <u>Absolutely</u>. On the sculpture, the letters are NYPVTT. When decoded, the letters read BERLIN.

Tony: I can't imagine being a code breaker, can you? I wouldn't be able to sleep because I'd be thinking about it all the time.

Gerald: That's exactly what's happening. Lots of people are obsessed with cracking the code and that's all they can think about every day.

Tony: <u>That's ridiculous</u>.

1 Gerald is really interested in Kryptos.	T	F
2 Gerald found out about Kryptos before Tony.	T	F
3 Tony knew about the new clues that the creator gave out.	T	F
4 Tony thinks a code breaker probably doesn't sleep much.	T	F

6 Match the expressions to the sentences. Write the letter.

___ **1** I'm hooked on it.

___ **2** Cool stuff.

___ **3** Absolutely.

___ **4** That's ridiculous.

a I agree with you completely.

b That's crazy. It's unreasonable.

c I'm obsessed with it.

d Interesting things.

3:09

7 Complete the dialogues with the expressions in 6. Then listen and check.

1 A: Jennifer's always reading.

   B: I know. She's _____ historical mysteries. She reads all day, every day!

   A: Really? _____.

2 A: There's a craft fair on Saturday. Let's go. They've always got such _____, haven't they?

   B: _____. I could buy everything. Brilliant idea!

Language in Action

AFFIRMATIVE STATEMENTS	NEGATIVE TAGS	NEGATIVE STATEMENTS	POSITIVE TAGS
The geoglyphs **are** in Peru, Experts **have** explained them, We **solved** the mystery,	**aren't** they? **haven't** they? **didn't** we?	Atlantis **isn't** real, Scientists **haven't** found it, It **didn't** make sense,	**is** it? **have** they? **did** it?

8 Complete the sentences with the correct question tags.

1 The Voynich manuscript is a mystery, _____?

2 The plants in the manuscript aren't real species, _____?

3 Scientists can't work out the language in the manuscript, _____?

4 The pictures of the plants are beautiful, _____?

5 The manuscript isn't a hoax, _____?

6 People can find a lot of information about the Voynich manuscript online, _____?

9 Complete the sentences. Write question tags.

1 Scientists haven't found an explanation for the crop circles in England, _____?

2 The crop circles have got perfect geometric patterns, _____?

3 The crop circle appeared in that field overnight, _____?

4 Proof for the theory that aliens created crop circles doesn't exist, _____?

10 Unscramble the sentences. Write question tags.

1   don't / some people / in the Bermuda Triangle / do / believe / they

_____

2   don't / a mysterious / people / phenomenon / love / they

_____

3   didn't / the Nazca Lines / learnt / we / a lot about / my classmates and I

_____

4   didn't / a theory for the Sailing Stones / did / scientists / have / for a long time / they

_____

5   seem / the city of Atlantis / does / doesn't / real / it

_____

11 Zack is writing a play about Atlantis. Help him complete the play. Use the question tags in the box.

> didn't they?   don't we?   do they?
> isn't it?   wasn't he?   were they?

Tabitha: Well, here we are in the city of Atlantis! Wow! It's really cool,
1 _____

Brian: Yeah. Look at that huge water fountain! It's beautiful!

Tabitha: We look a little funny wearing jeans and T-shirts,
2 _____

Brian: I told you that we'd look strange. Look at that wall. It's covered in gold and silver!

Tabitha: All the walls are covered in metals. Scientists don't really know why this place disappeared, ³_____

Brian: No, but Plato seemed to know. He said that the gods destroyed Atlantis.

Tabitha: Right. The people weren't good, ⁴_____ So the gods destroyed the city with an earthquake and giant waves, ⁵_____

Brian: That's right. Hey, look at that hill. Why is there a hill in the middle of the city?

Tabitha: Look at the top.

Brian: Oh, that's right. That's the temple of Poseidon. He was a very scary god,
6 _____

Tabitha: Absolutely. It's brilliant to travel back in time.

3:11

12 Listen and read. Who thought the lights came from a god?

What Causes the Aurora Borealis?

The aurora borealis, whose colours light up the night sky, is one of the most beautiful phenomena on Earth. It is also one of the most mystifying since every display of shimmering colours, lines and shapes is different each time it appears. Long ago, people in Finland thought the lights came from a mystical fox flashing its tail in the sky. The Algonquin tribe in Canada thought that the lights came from the god that created them. They believed that after the god finished, he went up north to live. The god showed his love for his people by making large spectacular fires that his people could see and enjoy.

Then in 2008, scientists developed a theory that everyone could agree on. The spectacular lights were caused by the solar wind blowing around ions, atoms, gases and other things in the atmosphere and making them collide. When they collided, they produced the colourful displays of light. So, how does it actually happen? The exact process is complicated but perhaps this simple diagram can help.

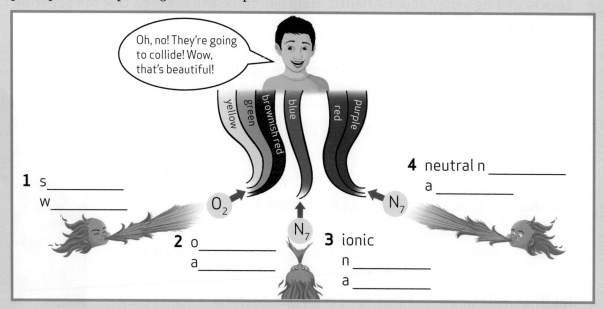

The hot solar winds from the sun are blowing the oxygen and two nitrogen atoms around. The atoms are full of energy. When they collide, they give off colours. Oxygen produces a yellow-green to brownish red colour. The two nitrogen atoms produce different colours. Ionic nitrogen atoms produce a blue colour. Neutral nitrogen atoms produce red and purple colours.

This is a simple explanation of how the aurora borealis is made. It's good to understand the science behind the phenomenon but the myths are fun to know, too, aren't they?

13 Read 12 again and complete the diagram. Use the words in the box.

> atom (3)   nitrogen (2)   oxygen   solar winds

14 Read. What colour is a yeti's fur?

Huge, Hairy Ape-like Creatures: Real or Hoax?

Huge, hairy ape-like creatures have been the 'stars' of at least ten films in Hollywood over the years. In some films, the hairy creature is friendly and huggable like a teddy bear. In other films, it's a terrifying beast that wants to destroy everyone and everything. In real life, this creature has got several names, depending on which region of the world it's seen in. In the United States and Canada, the creature is called Bigfoot or Sasquatch. In the Himalayan regions of Asia, it's called the *yeti* or the abominable snowman. The colour of the fur may be different (the yeti has usually got white fur and Bigfoot has got dark brown or black) but they both appear to be up to 2.7 metres tall and weigh from 300 to 400 kilos. Their feet can be as large as 43 centimetres long. But are these creatures real?

For years, scientists have thought that these creatures were a hoax but to this day people continue to claim that they've seen them. In 2012, there were many sightings in the United States. One person posted his video on YouTube and the video was seen more than 2 million times.

A theory of some scientists is that the creature is a Gigantopithecus, a giant ape-like species that scientists thought was extinct. There hasn't been any proof for this theory, but the mystery may soon be solved. Scientists think they've got some DNA samples from sightings. If the tests are positive, then the mystery creatures will finally become part of the amazing, fascinating world of science. If they're negative, these creatures will be part of myths and legends. Whatever the result, it seems clear that these creatures will continue to appear in real-life sightings, in stories and in films. Why? Because we love mystery and fantasy and we love to be surprised – at times, even frightened! – by the world around us.

15 Read 14 again and answer the questions.

1 Scientists think that the yeti and Bigfoot are the same creature. Why do you think they look different in different regions of the earth?

2 Do you like watching films that have got creatures like Bigfoot or the yeti in them? Why/ Why not?

THINK BIG

Do you think the yeti exists? Why/Why not?

_____

One purpose for writing is to explain something. When you write a cause-and-effect paragraph, you explain *why* something happens.

- Why something happens is called a **cause**.
- The thing that happens is called an **effect**.

For example, the aurora borealis is a beautiful display of lights. The beautiful lights are an effect. Why do the lights happen? That's the cause.

16 Read the paragraph. <u>Underline</u> the causes. (Circle) the effects.

> The aurora borealis is a brilliant light show. Coloured bands of light paint the night sky in certain parts of the world. What makes this happen? Solar winds interact with the upper part of the atmosphere, causing atoms of oxygen and nitrogen to become changed. As the atoms return to their normal state, they give off colours.

17 Write a cause-and-effect paragraph about something that's happened to you or something you've read about in your Science lessons. Use the chart below to organise your ideas.

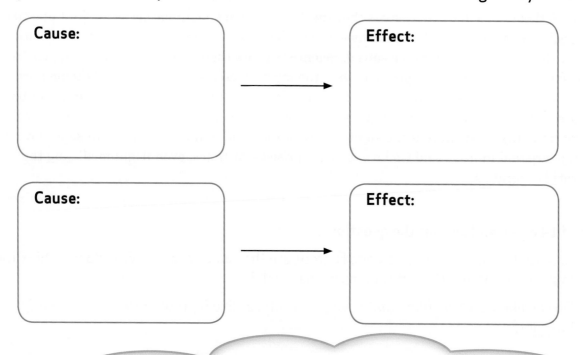

Cause:

Effect:

Cause:

Effect:

THINK BIG If you could ask a scientist any question about why something happens, what would you ask?

_____

18 **Complete the sentences. Circle the answers.**

1 There is no ___ for planes and boats disappearing in the Bermuda Triangle.

   a explanation   **b** phenomenon

2 Scientists know how the Sailing Stones move. That mystery is ___.

   a solved   **b** unsolved

3 Scientists think that crop circles are a hoax. This is a ___.

   a proof   **b** theory

4 Code breakers won't stop trying to crack the code until they've got ___ proof that the Voynich manuscript really is a hoax.

   a solved   **b** scientific

19 **Correct the question tags.**

1 The aurora borealis is a phenomenon in the northern hemisphere, is it?

_____

2 The yeti lives in the Himalayas in Asia, isn't it?

_____

3 There's proof that the Sailing Stones are real, aren't there?

_____

4 The man who designed Kryptos wanted to challenge code breakers, didn't they?

_____

5 Kryptos isn't a video game, isn't it?

_____

20 **Complete the dialogues. Use question tags. Use the information you have learnt about mysteries.**

A: _____?

B: Yes, they are! That's true!

A: _____?

B: Yes, it is. I agree! Absolutely!

WHY IS IT FAMOUS?

1 Do you recognise these places? Match the descriptions to the pictures. Write the numbers. Why are these places famous? What do you think? Circle 1 for architecture, 2 for natural beauty or 3 for mystery. You can circle more than one.

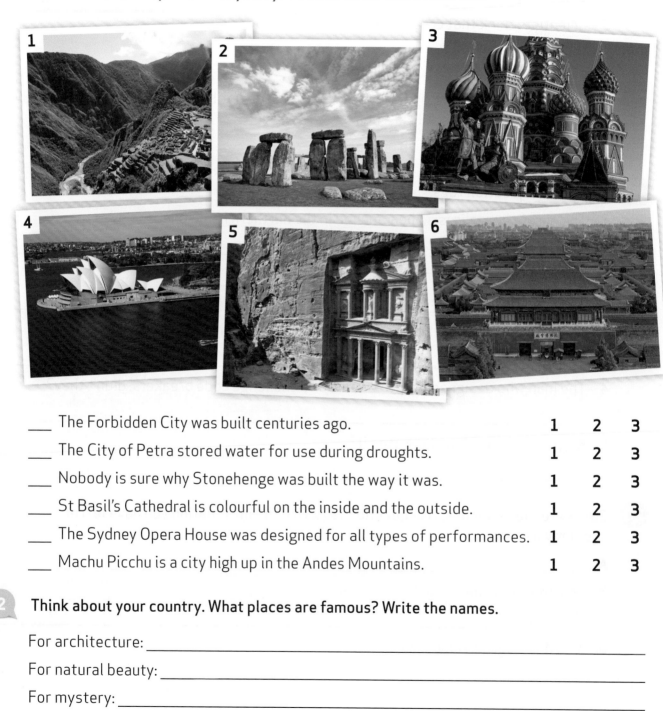

___ The Forbidden City was built centuries ago.	1	2	3
___ The City of Petra stored water for use during droughts.	1	2	3
___ Nobody is sure why Stonehenge was built the way it was.	1	2	3
___ St Basil's Cathedral is colourful on the inside and the outside.	1	2	3
___ The Sydney Opera House was designed for all types of performances.	1	2	3
___ Machu Picchu is a city high up in the Andes Mountains.	1	2	3

2 Think about your country. What places are famous? Write the names.

For architecture: _____

For natural beauty: _____

For mystery: _____

3 Listen and label the pictures with the words from the box.

mausoleum	monument	pyramid
statue	temple	tower

1 _____

2 _____

3 _____

4 _____

5 _____

6 _____

4 Answer the questions.

1 Look at **3**. If your class could travel to one of the places or structures, which one would you like to see?

_____

2 Have you ever visited a historic place like those pictured? What do you remember most about that place?

_____

_____

Does a landmark have to be old to be famous? Why/Why not?

THINK BIG

_____

_____

5 Listen and read. Then answer the questions.

The Forbidden City

In the middle of Beijing, China, is the magnificent Forbidden City. Although now a museum and officially renamed the Palace Museum, or 'Gugong' in Chinese, the Forbidden City was built in the early 1400s by Emperor Yongle as his imperial home. With 90 palaces and over 900 buildings, the Forbidden City was home to 24 Chinese emperors of the Ming and Qing dynasty for almost 500 years.

The Forbidden City is protected by a moat and a wall that is almost 8 metres high. There is an inner court with buildings and rooms for the emperor and his family and an outer court with halls and gardens where the emperor did his work and entertained guests. Only people invited by the emperor were allowed into the palace. All others were forbidden to enter.

In front of the main gate, there is a pair of bronze lions. The male lion is holding a globe, symbolising the power of the emperor. The female lion has got a cub. She symbolises the health and happiness of the emperor's family.

The colours yellow and red appear everywhere. Roofs of the buildings and bricks of the floor are yellow. Yellow symbolised the royal family and its supreme importance to the world. Doors, windows, pillars and walls were often red. Red symbolised happiness and celebration.

Today, people come from all over the world to see the thousands of items in the Palace Museum: paintings, ceramics, jade pieces, clocks, jewellery and sculptures – all give us a glimpse of history. In 1987, the United Nations Educational, Scientific and Cultural Organization (UNESCO) included the Forbidden City on its World Heritage List for its incredible architectural beauty and wealth of cultural artefacts.

1 When was the Forbidden City built? Why was it built?

_____

2 Why do you think the emperor's palace was called the Forbidden City?

_____

3 There are statues of lions in front of the main gate. If you lived in a place like the Forbidden City, what animal statues would you have in front of your main gate? Why?

_____

4 The colours red and yellow appear everywhere in the Forbidden City. If you lived in a place like the Forbidden City, what two colours would you use? What would they symbolise?

_____

3:24

6 Listen and read. Then answer the question.

Tania: Hi, Eric! You're from Australia, aren't you?

Eric: Yes, I was born in Sydney. Why?

Tania: Well, I've got to give a presentation in my Art class. What do you know about the Sydney Opera House?

Eric: Quite a lot, actually. Did you know that the Opera House is <u>known for</u> its design?

Tania: Hmm. <u>That makes sense</u>. I've seen pictures and it's amazing, isn't it?

Eric: Yeah, it's a <u>work of art</u>! I don't know who designed it but I do know where the person was from. A design contest <u>was held</u> sometime in the 1950s and the person who won was from Denmark.

Tania: Really? You know, it looks like a big boat, doesn't it?

Eric: Yeah, I've heard other people say the same thing. It's amazing!

Tania: Thanks, Eric. You've given me a good start.

Do Tania and Eric like the design of the Opera House? How do you know?

_____

7 Look at 6. Read the underlined expressions. How can you say them in other words? Match the expressions. Write the letter.

___ **1** known for   **a** happened or took place

___ **2** That makes sense.   **b** painting, sculpture or object that is skillfully made

___ **3** work of art   **c** famous for

___ **4** was held   **d** That's logical. It's easy to understand.

3:25

8 Complete the dialogues with the expressions in 7. Then listen and check.

1 A: My family is going to the city of Cambridge this weekend.

   B: Really? I've heard of it but I don't know much about it.

   A: It's _____ its architecture and its university, of course. You should go!

2 A: How was your holiday in Paris?

   B: Great! We saw the Eiffel Tower. It's a phenomenal _____!

3 A: I'm doing research on Machu Picchu since we're going there on our next holiday.

   B: _____.

Active	Passive
Archaeologists discovered Machu Picchu in 1911.	Machu Picchu **was discovered** in 1911 (by archaeologists).

9 Complete the sentences with the passive form of the verb in brackets and is/are.

1 The Galapagos Islands _____ (know) for their unique variety of animal and plant species.

2 The Forbidden City _____ (fill) with beautiful paintings and artefacts.

3 The Taj Mahal _____ (make) of marble.

4 The walls of the Taj Mahal _____ (decorate) with many floral designs.

5 The inside walls of St Basil's Cathedral _____ (paint) every few years.

6 The Sydney Opera House _____ (locate) in Australia.

10 Next to each sentence, write A for active or P for passive.

___ 1 Easter Island was discovered by Dutch explorers in 1722.

___ 2 It's still not known why the Moai statues on Easter Island were created.

___ 3 Trees were probably used to move the statues on Easter Island.

___ 4 Ivan the Terrible built St Basil's Cathedral in Moscow in the mid-16th century.

___ 5 The city of Petra was constructed sometime around the 4th century BC.

___ 6 A Danish architect designed the Sydney Opera House.

11 Write sentences with the passive form of the verbs in brackets.

1 (call) El Castillo / the Pyramid at Kukulcán

_____

2 (rebuild) some of the stones of Stonehenge / in the early 20th century

_____

3 (give) The Statue of Liberty / to the United States as a gift

_____

> Leonardo da Vinci is the famous artist and inventor **who painted** the Mona Lisa.
> The Eiffel Tower is a landmark **that has become** the symbol of Paris, France.

12 **Write who or that.**

1 The Galapagos Islands are named after the huge tortoises _____ are native to the island.

2 Charles Darwin studied the plants and animals _____ lived on the Galapagos Islands in the early 1800s.

3 It was Charles Darwin _____ made the Islands famous.

4 The tortoises and lizards aren't afraid of the visitors _____ come to see them.

5 The animal _____ is the best known of all is the Galapagos Tortoise.

13 **Match the sentences. Write the letters.**

____ **1** Machu Picchu is an ancient city.

____ **2** Many tourists get to Machu Picchu by walking on paths.

____ **3** Scientists don't know much about the Inca.

____ **4** Scientists know about the Spanish conquerors.

a They invaded the city in the 1500s.

b The city was built high in the Andes Mountains.

c The Inca lived in Machu Picchu long ago.

d The paths lead to the ancient city.

14 **Look at 13. Rewrite the matched sentences as one sentence. Use who or that.**

1 _____

2 _____

3 _____

4 _____

15 Listen and read. Where was the farmer who lost his hammer?

ACCIDENTAL DISCOVERIES

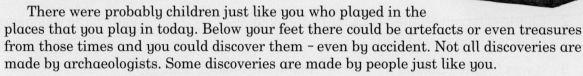

Do you ever wonder what the world around you looked like hundreds or even thousands of years ago? What do you know about the cultures and people that used to live where you live now?

There were probably children just like you who played in the places that you play in today. Below your feet there could be artefacts or even treasures from those times and you could discover them – even by accident. Not all discoveries are made by archaeologists. Some discoveries are made by people just like you.

One important accidental discovery occurred in 1992, in England. A farmer was working in the fields when he lost his hammer. He asked a neighbour to help him find it. His neighbour had a metal detector. The first thing the metal detector found was a silver spoon. Then it found some jewellery and gold coins. The surprised farmers asked for the help of archaeologists. When the archaeologists came, they were shocked to discover a large box with over 14,000 Roman gold and silver coins inside. They believed that the treasure came from the 4th and 5th centuries BC. The archaeologists found other artefacts as well, including the farmer's hammer. The artefacts were sold to museums and the farmers received 2.5 million pounds!

In another accidental discovery, workers in Wyoming, in the United States, were digging up land to make a football field. They discovered artefacts from an ancient village that existed as long ago as the 1st century AD.

Do you think the past is just waiting for you to uncover it? It may be. So, the next time you walk out of your door, look carefully at the world around you. You never know what you might find.

16 Read 15 again and answer the questions.

1 What did the farmer discover?

_____

2 What did archaeologists believe?

_____

3 What accidental discovery was made in Wyoming?

_____

THINK BIG

Pretend the year is 2500. Make a list of three everyday objects that you want archaeologists to find and say why each object is important in your life.

_____

_____

17 Read. How many criteria were used to choose the new seven wonders?

The New 7 Wonders of the World

    Over two thousand years ago in ancient Greece, an engineer, Philon of Byzantium, created a list of the Seven Ancient Wonders of the World. Today, only one of those wonders still exists: the pyramids of Egypt. In 1999, Bernard Weber, a Swiss adventurer, decided to create a new list of world wonders. He began the New 7 Wonders Foundation. This time, he wanted people from all around the world to choose the seven new wonders that exist today. He asked people to send in their votes for the new wonders. People voted by texting, voting online on the website and calling in their votes. By 2007, more than 100 million people had voted. Who were these voters? Most of the voters were not adults. Bernard Weber is proud of the fact that they were mostly children and young people.

    Weber and a group of people reviewed all the votes. They chose the new seven wonders based on these criteria:

- The places should each have a unique beauty.
- The places should come from all over the world and represent people from all over the world.
- The places should be from different environments, such as deserts and rainforests.
- The places should be important to people from different cultures.
- The places should be located on many continents.

    The final list of seven new wonders was decided. They are described on page 101 of your Pupil's Book. Weber was delighted by the enthusiasm and love that people showed for their cultures and other cultures. This enthusiasm and love, he believes, creates a feeling of hope for the future.

18 Read 17 again and answer the questions.

1 Who began the New 7 Wonders Foundation?

_____

2 Who voted for the new seven wonders?

_____

3 What does Weber say creates a feeling of hope for the future?

_____

19 Pretend that you have to choose seven special places in your town or city. Which seven places are important to you, your family and friends? Write about them and say why.

_____

_____

When you do research for a report, use an idea web to organise the information into categories. For example, if you write about a country, make categories for its location, population and important cities.

When you write, make sure that you write only about one category of information in each paragraph.

20 Look at the facts. Write the number of each fact in the correct category.

1   between Pakistan and Burma

2   Kolkata, Chennai, Bangalore, Mumbai

3   southern Asia

4   Hindi

5   English – important language

6   New Delhi – capital city

7   one billion people

8   seventh largest country in the world

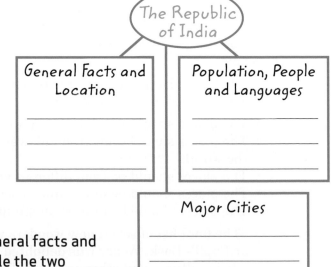

21 The paragraph below should only include general facts and information about the location of India. Circle the two sentences that do NOT belong in the paragraph.

The Republic of India is the seventh largest country in the world. It's located in southern Asia. Hindi is its national language. It's situated between Pakistan and Burma. It's the seventh largest country in the world. English is an important language, too.

22 Write a report about India. Write three paragraphs. In paragraph 1, write about general facts and location. In paragraph 2, write about major cities. In paragraph 3, write about population, people and languages. Use information in 20 and 21. Add information from your own research and your own idea web.

THINK BIG

What makes a country a good/bad place to live in? Why?

_____

_____

23 **Complete the sentences. Circle the letters.**

1 A ___ is a place that's built for someone who has died.

   a tower   **b** mausoleum

2 The French gave the United States a ___ as a sign of friendship.

   a statue   **b** palace

3 There are famous ___ in both Egypt and Mexico.

   a mausoleums   **b** pyramids

4 In Indonesia, there is a ___ that contains more than 500 statues of the Buddha.

   a mausoleum   **b** temple

24 **Complete the statements with the passive form of the verbs in the box.**

> build   discover   locate   make   use

1 The Temple of Borobudur _____ by thousands of workers between 750 and 850 AD.

2 The Taj Mahal _____ in Agra, India.

3 The Taj Mahal _____ of white marble.

4 Victoria Falls _____ by David Livingstone in 1855.

5 Some scientists believe that ropes _____ to pull the large Moai Statues across Easter Island.

25 **Combine the sentences. Use that or who and the sentences in the box.**

> They belonged to King Tutankhamen.
> They helped to construct the Taj Mahal.
> They lived on Easter Island.

1 In Agra, India, there were more than 22,000 people.

   _____.

2 The Rapa Nui are Polynesian people.

   _____.

3 In the Cairo Museum in Egypt are artefacts.

   _____.

unit 9 THAT'S ENTERTAINMENT!

1 Read the statements. Circle the ones that describe you.

1 Music is very important in my life.

2 Reading is very important in my life.

3 Video games are very important in my life.

4 Films are very important in my life.

5 I like reading about singers and actors.

6 I like animation more than regular films.

7 I like films that scare me.

8 I like talking about the concerts I go to.

2 Read and circle.

	Sometimes	Often	Never
1 I go to the cinema.	S	O	N
2 I go to live concerts.	S	O	N
3 I go to bookshops or the library.	S	O	N
4 I go to festivals to see people perform.	S	O	N
5 I watch film award programmes on TV.	S	O	N
6 I watch music contests on TV.	S	O	N
7 I read when I get bored.	S	O	N
8 I play video games when I get bored.	S	O	N

Complete the sentences. Use the words in the box.

book signing   comic book exhibition   concert
festival   film premiere   video game launch

1 People are walking around dressed up as Star Wars storm troopers, Avatar characters and Mario. There are cool books, posters, T-shirts and hats for sale. Going to a _____ is so much fun!

2 People are standing in a queue waiting until midnight to get into the shop. Everybody wants to be the first to own the new game. This _____ is the best!

3 The place is full of people dancing and singing along with the performer on stage. The music is really loud! The tickets were expensive but worth it to see this singer in _____!

4 Photographers are taking pictures of the actors as they walk into the cinema. People are so excited to see their favourite stars! Being at a _____ is incredible!

5 The author of the latest best-selling book is sitting behind a table. People are standing in a queue holding the book. A _____ is really fun to go to.

6 Thousands of people have come to see the dancers dressed in stunning traditional costumes dancing to folk music. People are in a wonderful mood for these two days at the _____.

 THINK BIG

If you went to a comic book exhibition and you could dress as any character, which character would you be? Why?

_____

_____

4 Read and listen. Then read the statements and circle the correct names.

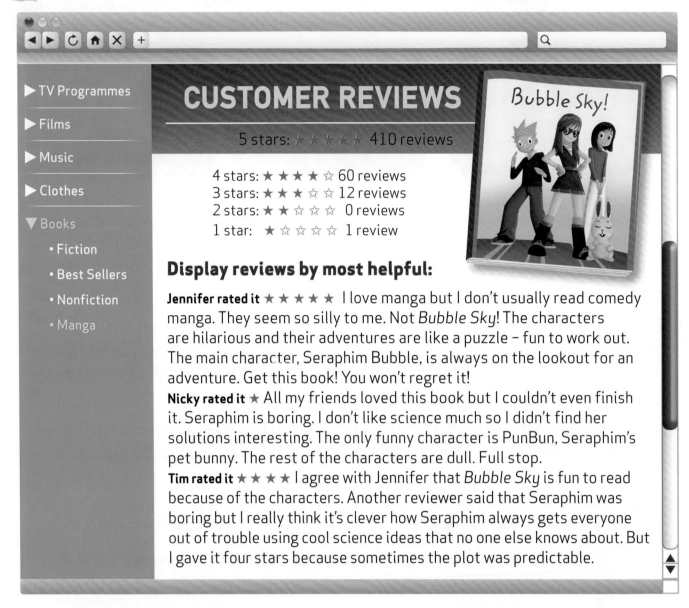

▶ TV Programmes

▶ Films

▶ Music

▶ Clothes

▼ Books
  • Fiction
  • Best Sellers
  • Nonfiction
  • Manga

CUSTOMER REVIEWS

Bubble Sky!

5 stars: ★ ★ ★ ★ ★ 410 reviews

4 stars: ★ ★ ★ ☆ 60 reviews
3 stars: ★ ★ ★ ☆ ☆ 12 reviews
2 stars: ★ ★ ☆ ☆ ☆ 0 reviews
1 star: ★ ☆ ☆ ☆ ☆ 1 review

Display reviews by most helpful:

Jennifer rated it ★ ★ ★ ★ ★ I love manga but I don't usually read comedy manga. They seem so silly to me. Not *Bubble Sky*! The characters are hilarious and their adventures are like a puzzle – fun to work out. The main character, Seraphim Bubble, is always on the lookout for an adventure. Get this book! You won't regret it!

Nicky rated it ★ All my friends loved this book but I couldn't even finish it. Seraphim is boring. I don't like science much so I didn't find her solutions interesting. The only funny character is PunBun, Seraphim's pet bunny. The rest of the characters are dull. Full stop.

Tim rated it ★ ★ ★ ★ I agree with Jennifer that *Bubble Sky* is fun to read because of the characters. Another reviewer said that Seraphim was boring but I really think it's clever how Seraphim always gets everyone out of trouble using cool science ideas that no one else knows about. But I gave it four stars because sometimes the plot was predictable.

1 **Jennifer / Nicky / Tim** said that the characters were hilarious.

2 **Jennifer / Nicky / Tim** said that all her friends loved the book.

3 **Jennifer / Nicky / Tim** said that the plot was sometimes predictable.

5 Answer the questions.

1 Why did Jennifer like the adventures?

_____

2 Have you ever read manga? What would a manga book need to include for you to give it five stars?

_____

4:07

6 Listen and read. Then answer the questions.

Ann: Mum? Um, could I possibly borrow ten pounds?

Mum: <u>What for</u>?

Ann: I want to go and see all the celebrities at the film premiere of Spider-Man. All my friends are going. But I haven't got enough money for the train.

Mum: What happened to your pocket money?

Ann: I spent it on going to that concert last week. It was more expensive than I thought.

Mum: Well, I suppose I could give you next week's pocket money <u>in advance</u> but that means you won't get anything next week.

Ann: OK. <u>Deal</u>! Thanks, Mum.

```
PREMIERE
SPIDER-MAN
```

1 What does Ann want from her mum?

_____

2 Ann won't get any pocket money next week. Why?

_____

7 Look at 6. Circle the correct answers.

1 When Mum says "What for?" she means ___.

  a Why do you need it?   **b** What do you mean?

2 "In advance" means ___.

  a an increase   **b** early

3 When Ann says "Deal!" she means ___.

  a I agree.   **b** Let's play cards.

4:08

8 Complete the dialogue with the underlined expressions in 6. Listen and check your answers.

John: Do you want to stop at the shopping centre on the way home?

Jim: ¹_____

John: I need some things for my science project.

Jim: OK. But only if we go to the pizza place in there first. I'm so hungry!

John: OK. ²_____

Language in Action

Direct speech	Reported speech
Claire said, "The album **isn't** as good as the last one."	Claire said (that) the album **wasn't** as good as the last one.
Josh said, "**I'm going** to the premiere."	Josh said (that) he **was going** to the premiere.

9 Read the dialogues and answer the questions. Use reported speech.

Katie: Hey, Joe! What are you doing tonight?

Joe: I'm going to a live concert at Dragon's Den to see One Direction. What about you?

Katie: I'm not doing anything.

1 What's Joe doing tonight?

_____

2 What's Katie doing tonight?

_____

Sam: The new *Play to Win 2* video game is really challenging.

Joanne: It's much better than *Play to Win 1*.

3 What did Sam say about *Play to Win 2*?

_____

4 What did Joanne say about *Play to Win 2*?

_____

Nina: I want to go to the comic book exhibition!

John: Me, too! I'm going to dress up as Mario.

5 Where did Nina want to go?

_____

6 What did John say?

_____

10 Read the dialogue and complete the sentences. Use reported speech.

> I don't want to miss the book signing at the bookshop today. My mum's taking me.

> I'm very excited. I'm going with my friend to a video game launch today!

1 He _____ he _____ to miss the book signing.

2 He _____ his mum _____ him.

3 She _____ she _____ very excited.

4 She _____ she _____ to a video game launch.

11 Read the dialogue and answer the questions. Use reported speech.

Janet: Hi, Charles. Where are you going?

Charles: I'm going to the cinema with a friend.

Janet: You're lucky. My friend doesn't want to go with me. I don't want to go by myself. But I really want to see the new *Bubble Sky* film.

Charles: Come with us.

Janet: Seriously? Thanks!

1 What did Charles say about his plans?

_____

2 What did Janet say about her friend?

_____

3 What did she say about going to the cinema by herself?

_____

4 What did she say she wanted to do?

_____

4:10

12 Listen and read. For how long have MMOs been popular?

Video Games: The Year 2000 and Now

The changes to the computer and video games industry since the year 2000 have been incredible. New technology has changed how, where and what people play, as well as who they play with. We've got a lot more choices now than we used to.

How People Play and Who They Play With

In the year 2000, people played on game consoles, desktop computers or in arcades. When they wanted to play with others they invited them over to their house, or they played alone. Some online games were available at the end of the 1990s but they were expensive and not as many people had access to the internet. Today, people can play games anywhere they want on portable gaming devices, phones or tablets. They can play online with friends or even with other players from around the world.

What People Play

Games today have got graphics that are sharper and more lifelike than they used to be and new technology has made games more challenging, with more variety. Since 2000, Massively Multi-player Online games (MMOs) have become popular. People like to compete against each other for higher scores. They love virtual worlds that offer experiences they could never have in real life. Dancing and exercise games and sports and adventure games have also become more popular.

This trend towards more choices and deeper involvement in virtual worlds will continue to change video games well into the future.

13 Read 12 again and answer the questions.

1 How is playing video games in 2000 different from playing video games today?

_____

2 Why do people like MMO games?

_____

3 Have you got a favourite video game? What is it? Why do you like it?

_____

THINK BIG

Some people feel that video games are bad for young people. Do you agree or disagree? Why?

_____

_____

14 Read. How many musicians are in the Vienna Vegetable Orchestra?

Unique Musical Instruments

Every culture has got musical instruments that are unique to its culture. The instruments are often made from a variety of materials such as wood, steel, animal bones and plastic. There's an orchestra in Vienna that's really unique because it plays instruments made from the things your mother tells you to eat every day. The Vienna Vegetable Orchestra plays instruments made out of vegetables.

The eleven musicians in the Vienna Vegetable Orchestra play carrot flutes, radish horns, pepper rattlers, carrot trumpets, aubergine clappers, pumpkin bongos and cucumber phones. The orchestra plays contemporary music, jazz and electronic music, among others. They've been playing together since 1998. They play concerts around the world. At the end of their concerts, the members of the audience receive a bowl of vegetable soup to enjoy. Their third album is called *Onionoise* and includes songs entitled 'Nightshades' and 'Transplants'.

Why did this group of visual artists, poets, designers and writers choose vegetables to create music? They were fascinated by the challenge to produce musical sounds using natural foods. They constantly experiment with vegetables to create new sounds. As part of their work, they give workshops on how to create instruments from vegetables. A morning TV programme said it was "…a highly unusual, tasty musical performance."

You knew vegetables were good for you. Now you know that they sound good, too!

15 Read 14 again and answer the questions.

1 Would you go to a Vienna Vegetable Orchestra concert? Why/Why not?

_____

_____

2 If you could play one of the vegetable instruments, which one would you like to play? Why?

_____

_____

3 Read the list of instruments again. Think of two other vegetables that the Vienna Vegetable Orchestra could use to make instruments. Say why.

_____

_____

A good film review briefly describes the important parts of the film: the story, the hero and characters and your opinion (what you liked and didn't like).

Before you write, make a chart that includes these topics and add vivid adjectives such as *stunning*, *captivating*, *tense*, *dull* and *boring*.

When you write, order your ideas. Write about the story first but don't give away the ending! Some people want the ending to be a surprise. Then write about the characters. Describe them and what they do. Finally, describe what you liked and didn't like (for example, the acting or special effects).

16 Put the paragraphs in order. Write 1, 2 or 3.

Review of *Bubble Sky: the Film*

____ Some of the acting is fabulous! Melinda Mendez is very good as Seraphim Bubble. Brad Davis is hilarious as Tran. The evil Ms Doze, played by Vivian Bell, is captivating but Sandy Dennis as the teacher is dull. The special effects are stunning! All in all, this was a very cool film!

____ *Bubble Sky* is a captivating animation adventure. In the story, a young girl discovers that her school is taken over by aliens. She works out that a particular herb might destroy them. She needs to find the herb and then get the aliens to eat it.

____ Seraphim Bubble is the hero of the story. Her pet rabbit, PunBun, gives good advice. Seraphim's younger brother Tran and her friend Gayle help her fight the aliens.

17 Look at 16. Complete the chart about *Bubble Sky*.

The story	The hero and characters	The opinion (what you liked and didn't like)

18 Write a review of a film playing near you this weekend. Make a chart to help you.

19 Circle the correct events.

1 The author arrived late for the **film premiere / book signing**. The manager of the bookshop was upset because people were waiting.

2 My brother and I went to the **comic book exhibition / video game launch**. We dressed up as Mario and Pikachu. There were thousands of people there.

3 My town is having an arts and crafts **concert / festival**. For three days, painters, potters and jewellery makers will be selling their work.

4 This Friday night all the stars will be at the **film premiere / festival** of the new Superman film.

5 The **concert / launch** tickets for The Eyes go on sale next Tuesday. They'll sell out fast!

20 Read and correct the one mistake in each reported speech sentence.

1 **Carol:**   I'm tired.

   Reported speech: She says she was tired.

   _____

2 **Jason:**   I'm going to be at the launch tomorrow.

   Reported speech: He said he is going to be at the launch tomorrow.

   _____

3 **Diana:**   I want to meet the author of the book.

   Reported speech: She said she want to meet the author of the book.

   _____

4 **Will:**   I don't like sci-fi films.

   Reported speech: He said he doesn't like sci-fi films.

   _____

21 Write the sentences using reported speech.

1 **Lara:** I'm quite a good singer.

   _____

2 **Paul:** I don't want to go to the festival today.

   _____

THINK BIG

1 Look at the pictures. Complete the items. Add your own items on the extra lines.

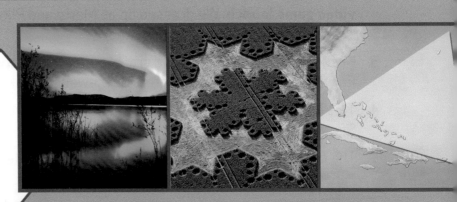

MYSTERIOUS EVENTS

1 Northern _____

2 _____ circles

3 Bermuda _____

4 _____

FAMOUS PLACES

1 _____ of Borobudur

2 _____ of Liberty

3 _____ of Kukulcán

4 _____

SPECIAL EVENTS

1 _____ signing

2 rock _____

3 film _____

4 _____

2 Find a famous place or event that interests you. Complete the chart.

Name of the place or event	_____
When was it built, discovered or found? When did it take place? Where is it located?	_____ _____
Is this a place or event that was mentioned in a song? What's the name of the song? Who's the singer? What are the lines (the lyrics) that mention the place?	_____ _____ _____ _____
This place or event was described in a book, online or in a magazine, wasn't it? What was the title of the book or article? What did the writer say about it?	_____ _____ _____

3 Do research. Find more information about the place or event that interests you in **2**. Write a report about the place or event.

_____

_____

_____

_____

_____

_____

_____

_____

1 Read Julia's plan for her Science report. Write questions and answers.
Use yet and already.

The Importance of the Monarch Butterfly
by Julia Black

Monday	Tuesday	Wednesday	Thursday	Friday
Morning: Go to Museum of Natural History, draw Monarch butterflies. Afternoon: Write questions about the butterflies.	Morning: Do research on Monarch butterflies and answer my questions.	Morning: Write my report on Monarch butterflies.	Morning: Create my presentation.	Morning: Hand in my report and give presentation.

1 *It's Monday afternoon.*

Q: (Julia / go to the museum) _____

A: _____

2 *It's Tuesday.*

Q: (write / her report) _____

A: _____

3 *It's Tuesday afternoon.*

Q: (she / do her research) _____

A: _____

4 *It's Thursday afternoon.*

Q: (she / create her presentation) _____

A: _____

5 *It's Thursday afternoon.*

Q: (she / give her presentation) _____

A: _____

1 Complete the sentences with the present perfect continuous form of the verbs and for or since.

1 Jimmy Woodard _____ (take) computers apart _____ he was five years old.

2 Caitlyn _____ (play) chess _____ she was very young.

3 Serena _____ (study) martial arts _____ five years.

4 I _____ (collect) stamps _____ two years.

2 Ask and answer questions about the chart. Use the present perfect and for or since.

Mr. Freedman's Class – Hobbies		
Pupil	Hobby	How Long?
Rob	collects coins	four years
Cynthia	makes jewellery	she was nine
David	draws cartoon characters	three years
Iris	has dance lessons	six months

1 How long _____
_____

2 How long _____
_____

3 _____
_____

4 _____
_____

1 Complete the sentences with the correct form of the verb in brackets.

How will you help your family and friends?

1 If I _____ (finish) my homework early, I'll help with the chores.

2 If my sister doesn't understand her homework, I _____ (help) her.

3 I _____ (call) my friend if he's ill.

4 If my dad _____ (ask) me to walk the dog, I _____ (do) it.

5 I _____ (tell) my parents if I _____ (break) something.

2 Complete the sentences.

1 If someone gives me a present, _____.

2 If someone in my family is ill, _____.

3 If my friend gets upset with me, _____.

4 If I don't feel well, _____.

3 Read and match. Write the letter.

Advice to a New Exchange Student at School

___ **1** You're new.

___ **2** Some people are mean to you.

___ **3** You don't speak the language well.

___ **4** You're always late for lessons.

a Get organised so that you get to lessons on time.

b Don't worry about your mistakes. Speak anyway.

c Join clubs so that you meet people.

d Stay away from those people.

4 Write the sentences in 3 with should or shouldn't.

1 _____

2 _____

3 _____

4 _____

5 Complete the sentences.

1 _____, you should ask them to stop.

2 _____, you should apologise.

3 _____, you should get help.

1 Read. Then circle the best answers.

	I like	I don't like
Emily	languages writing and blogging big families living close to family	sports
Al	making money all sports studying hard living in other countries	languages

1 In 10 years, **Emily / Al** will definitely be studying languages at university.

2 In 10 years, **Emily / Al** probably will be running and hiking at the weekends.

3 In 10 years, **Emily / Al** probably won't be living in the same city.

4 In 20 years, **Emily / Al** will definitely be running an international business.

5 In 20 years, **Emily / Al** probably will be writing books.

2 Read. Then complete the sentences with I'll be or I won't be and the words in brackets.

What will you be doing in 20 years?

1 Celia: I love animals. I don't like living in the city. I like travelling.

 a _____ (work as a vet)

 b _____ (live in the country)

 c _____ (go on holiday to the same place every year)

2 Jeff: I love biology and helping people. I don't like cooking. I like boats.

 a _____ (finish medical school)

 b _____ (work as a chef)

 c _____ (sail my boat)

3 Answer the questions about yourself. Use No, definitely not, Yes, definitely, Probably not or Yes, probably.

1 In seven years will you be at university? _____

2 In two years will you be blogging? _____

3 Next year will you be in Year 8? _____

1 Complete the dialogues. Use the phrases in the box.

> join some clubs   start a blog
> start reading fun things like manga comics   have lots of singing lessons

1 Rita: I want to be a singer when I grow up.

    Eddie: If I were you, _____.

2 John: I don't enjoy reading.

    Nancy: If I were you, _____.

3 Tom: I'm bored all the time.

    Kristy: If I were you, _____.

4 Grace: I like writing a lot.

    Sam: If I were you, _____.

2 Complete the sentences. Circle the correct verbs.

1 If you **will get / got** up earlier, you **wouldn't be / won't be** late for school all the time.

2 If the world **could have / can have** superheroes, it **would be / was** a safer place to live.

3 If he **practised / will practise** the guitar more, he **will play / would play** better.

4 If our chess team **will win / won** more matches, we **will compete / would compete** in the national championships.

3 Unscramble the phrases. Complete and answer the questions.

1 (live / could / you / if / anywhere)

    _____,

    where would you live?

    I _____.

2 (you / choose / which / would)
    If you could choose your own super powers,

    _____?

    I _____.

3 (didn't / if / have / computers / we)

    _____,

    what would we do?

    We _____.

1 Complete the sentences. Circle the correct words.

1 Pandas only live in China. Brown bears live in many countries. Pandas live in **more / fewer** places than brown bears.

2 Brown bears spend **less / more** time eating than pandas. Pandas need to eat lots of bamboo every day to get enough nutrients.

3 Parakeets have got **fewer / more** legs than dogs.

4 Parakeets eat **more / less** food than dogs.

2 Read the facts. Then complete the sentences using most, least or fewest and the words in brackets.

> **Facts**
> Monserrat has got <u>less</u> crime than other countries.
> Greater London has got <u>more</u> people than other counties in England.
> North America has got <u>more</u> meat-eating plants than any other continent.
> Canada has got very <u>few</u> species of mammals. It has got fewer than any other country.
> People in Papua, New Guinea, speak <u>more</u> languages than people in other countries.
> Taki Taki, the language of Suriname, has got <u>few</u> words.

1 Greater London has got the _____ of any other county in England. (people)

2 People in Papua, New Guinea, speak the _____ of any country. (languages)

3 Canada has got _____ of any country. (species of mammals)

4 North America has got the _____ of any continent. (meat-eating plants)

5 The language of Taki Taki has got the _____ of all languages. (words)

6 The country of Monserrat has got the _____ of all countries. (crime)

3 Write sentences with the words in the box. Use superlatives.

1 The sun bear lives in Southeast Asia. It is only 1.2 metres tall. It is _____ in the world.

2 No bird is taller than the ostrich. The ostrich is _____ in the world.

3 No animal on land is larger than the elephant. The elephant is _____ on land.

4 No animal is louder than the blue whale. The blue whale is _____ in the world.

> large / creature
> loud / animal
> small / bear
> tall / bird

1 **Complete the sentences. Write the correct words.**

1 Kryptos is a sculpture in the United States, _____ it?

    is   isn't

2 The fourth section of Kryptos isn't solved, _____ it?

    is   isn't

3 There are many people trying to solve it, _____ there?

    are   aren't

4 Code breakers can't solve it, _____ they?

    can   can't

5 Anyone can try to crack the code, _____ they?

    can   can't

2 **Write question tags to complete the questions.**

1 The Great Pyramids of Egypt are beautiful, _____?

2 The Sailing Stones aren't a mystery any more, _____?

3 The Bermuda Triangle is mysterious, _____?

4 You can climb the pyramids in Mexico, _____?

3 **Unscramble the sentences and add words to make question tags.**

1 found out / scientists / in the early 20th century / about the Nazca Lines

_____

2 the Nazcans created / the lines / don't / scientists / know why

_____

3 drew / the Nazcans / animal and plant figures

_____

4 the lines / need to see / you / from a plane

_____

5 didn't know / you / about the Nazca Lines

_____

1 **Complete the sentences. Circle the correct verbs.**

1 The Mona Lisa **paints** / **was painted** by Leonardo da Vinci.

2 The Taj Mahal **was built** / **built** by the emperor of India.

3 The Church of San Francisco de Asis in New Mexico
damaged / **was damaged** by an earthquake in 1906.

4 The Statue of Liberty and the Eiffel Tower **were designed** /
designed by the same French designer.

2 **Write these sentences in the passive.**

1 The people of Egypt built the Great Pyramids of Egypt.

_____

2 Someone moved the Moai statues of Easter Island.

_____

3 **Write sentences in the passive. Use the verbs in the box.**

> carve   destroy   name   trade

1 The city of Petra, Jordan / one of the seven wonders of the world in 2007

_____

2 The city of Petra / out of the sandstone mountains in the Jordan desert

_____

_____

3 Spices, perfumes and other things / in Petra

_____

_____

4 The city of Petra / by an earthquake in 363 AD / nearly

_____

_____

4 **Complete the sentences with the names of places in your country.**

1 _____ is visited every year by thousands of tourists.

2 _____ is known as one of the most beautiful places in my country.

3 _____ is said to be one of the most mysterious places in
my country.

1 What did the people say about the film?
Change the sentences to reported speech.

Claire: The acting is incredible.

Jeff: The music is really cool.

Mira: It isn't the director's best film.

Nancy: It's definitely going to win an Oscar.

Tom: It's not that entertaining.

1 Claire _____.

2 Jeff _____.

3 Mira _____.

4 Nancy _____.

5 Tom _____.

2 Change the sentences to reported speech.

Tina: I'm going to a Justin Bieber concert for my birthday.

Paul: I'm going to a film premiere to see Jennifer Lawrence.

1 Tina _____.

2 Paul _____.

Mike: I want to buy the new *Cats* video game.

Sheila: I don't like playing video games.

3 Mike _____.

4 Sheila _____.

Tonya: I'm not going to the book signing.

Freddie: I always go to book signings.

5 She _____.

6 He _____.

Young Learners English Practice
Flyers

Note to pupils:

These practice materials will help you prepare
for the YLE (Young Learners English) Tests.
There are three kinds of practice materials in this sampler:
Listening, Reading & Writing and Speaking.
Good luck!

Young Learner's English Practice Flyers: Listening A

– 5 questions –

 Listen and draw lines. There is one example.

Young Learner's English Practice Flyers: Listening B

– 5 questions –

 Listen and write. There is one example.

Interview with a Star

Career: _football player_

1 | **How many years:** _____ years

2 | **When playing in Olympics:** in _____ months

3 | **Olympic goal:** _____ medal

4 | **Plans in ten years:** _____

5 | **Message for young people:** _____

Young Learner's English Practice Flyers: Listening C

– 5 questions –

 Listen and tick (✔) the box. There is one example.

What time does the concert start?

A ☐

B ☑

C ☐

1   What subject did Mary choose for her History project?

A ☐

B ☐

C ☐

2   What did Tom buy?

A ☐

B ☐

C ☐

3 Which country would Bill like to visit?

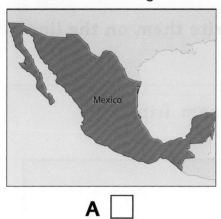

A ☐

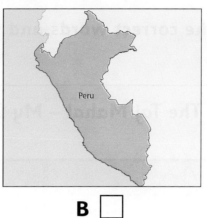

B ☐

C ☐

4 What homework is Katy going to do tonight?

$$a + b = c$$
$$a - b = d$$

A ☐

B ☐

C ☐

5 Which structure is Emma learning about?

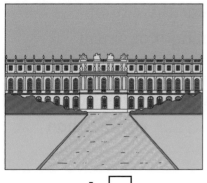

A ☐

B ☐

C ☐

Young Learner's English Practice Flyers: Reading & Writing A

– 8 questions –

Read the text. Choose the correct words and write them on the lines.

The Taj Mahal – My Dream Trip!

Example   If I _____could_____ visit anywhere in the world, I would love
to visit the Taj Mahal in India. The Taj Mahal is a gigantic

1   mausoleum that _____ by the emperor Shah Jahan

2   in memory of his wife. It _____ near the city of
Agra. I think it's got to be the most stunning monument

3   _____ can be found in India.

4   There are more _____ two million people who visit

5   the Taj Mahal every year. It gets _____ visitors than
Buckingham Palace in London.

6   My uncle visited the Taj Mahal last year and he _____
the weather was amazing and it was really beautiful. I haven't

7   saved enough money for my trip _____ but I can't wait

8   to go someday. If I could, I _____ go tomorrow!

Example	can	will	could
1	build	is building	was built
2	located	is located	was located
3	that	who	when
4	of	to	than
5	more	most	the most
6	said	tell	say
7	now	already	yet
8	do	would	will

Young Learner's English Practice Flyers: Reading & Writing B

– 5 questions –

Richard is talking to his friend, Harry. What does Harry say?

Read the conversation and choose the best answer. Write a letter (A–H) for each answer.

You do not need to use all the letters.

Example

> **Richard:** What are you doing this weekend?
>
> **Harry:** _____B_____.

Questions

1 **Richard:** What's your report about?

   Harry: _____

2 **Richard:** That's hard to write about, isn't it?

   Harry: _____

3 **Richard:** I haven't got any homework. I'm going to a football match on Sunday afternoon.

   Harry: _____

4 **Richard:** Maybe you can. Have you started your report yet?

   Harry: _____

5 **Richard:** Well, get busy. If you finish the report early, you can come with us.

   Harry: _____

A Good idea. I'll get started now.

B I have to finish a report by Monday. **(Example)**

C I don't think it's hard. It's interesting.

D I don't, do you?

E It's about life in the future.

F No, I haven't.

G If I were you, I'd get started straight away.

H I wish I could go with you.

Young Learner's English Practice Flyers: Reading & Writing C

– 7 questions –

Look at the picture and read the story. Write some words to complete the sentences about the story. You can use 1, 2, 3 or 4 words.

A Discovery in the Back Garden

My name's Robert and I've got an amazing story to tell. Most people don't believe me when I tell them about it but it's completely true.

One day, my friend Sarah brought a small potted tree to my house. My mum said it was OK for us to plant the tree in the back garden. While I was digging, I found something hard and round.

"What is it?" Sarah asked.

"I'm not sure," I said, "but I think it's a coin."

We brushed it off and looked at it more closely. It wasn't perfectly round and it wasn't very shiny but it was definitely a coin or a token of some kind. On one side was a picture of a man's face. He had a big nose and looked very serious. The word 'Roma' was printed on the other side.

Sarah thought it might be a bus token from Italy. We decided to take it to the museum. An expert looked at the coin. She said it was from ancient Rome. "You've discovered an important piece of history," she said.

"This is very mysterious," I said. "I wonder how it got into my back garden?"

Like I said, most people don't believe me when I tell this story. If you don't believe me, you can go to the museum and see the coin for yourself.

Examples

The person telling this story is called _____Robert_____.

Most people _____don't believe_____ him when he tells this story.

Questions

1 One day, Sarah brought a small _____ to Robert's house.

2 Robert's mum said it was OK to _____ in the back garden.

3 Robert found something that was _____ and round while he was digging.

4 On one side of the coin, there was a picture of _____.

5 On the other side of the coin, the word 'Roma' _____.

6 Robert went to _____ and spoke to an expert.

7 The expert said the discovery was an important _____.

MUSIC

ENGLISH

SCIENCE

ART

Young Learner's English Practice Flyers: Speaking B

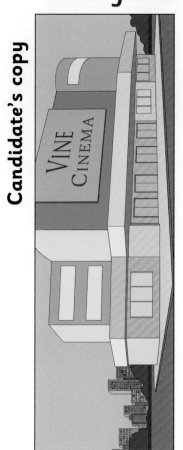

The Vine Cinema

Manager's name	?
How many / employees	?
What / food	?
Busy / not busy	?
What time / film starts	?

Information exchange

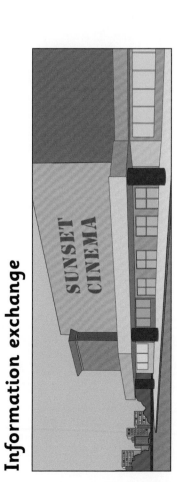

The Sunset Cinema

Manager's name	Mr Brown
How many / employees	5
What / food	ice cream and sweets
Busy / not busy	busy
What time / film starts	5:15

Pupil B

I need to buy some glue so I can finish my model.

I've been learning about the solar system in school and I like it.

Yes, I want to do a project about Pablo Picasso.

I need to write a report about him and make a big poster to show some of his works of art.

Yes, I want to do a project about the solar system.

Yes, I've written my report but I haven't built the model yet.

No, I haven't. I'm going to start looking at some websites about him on the internet.

I need to build a model of the solar system and write a report about it.

Yes, I need to buy some ink for our printer. I need to print out some of his paintings.

I've been learning about him in Art and I like his paintings.

Mystery Classmate: _____

(Remember: Don't read the name aloud!)

???

If this person could eat any food every day, it would be _____.

He/She plays more _____ than _____.

He/She reads fewer _____ than _____.

He/She definitely spends _____ time in front of the computer than some people I know.

If he/she didn't have to go to school every day, he/she would _____ and _____ from morning till night.

My classmate thinks he/she will probably be living in _____ in twenty years. And he'll/she'll probably be working as a(n) _____.

Who is he/she?

Description cards

One set for the group leader   *One set for each group*

International Mystery Solvers

It's a new video game about explorers…

…who are trying to solve the mystery of a lost island civilisation.

Chasing Bigfoot

It's a new comic book about a team of explorers…

…who travel by boat and plane into a danger zone in search of answers.

Return to Atlantis

It's a new film about a group of scientists…

…who are looking for a giant, mysterious creature that lives in the forests of North America.

Inside the Bermuda Triangle

It's a new sci-fi book about some scientists…

…who go from country to country searching for answers to the world's most hard-to-solve mysteries.

Review cards

One set for each group member

Your best friend says, "It's amazing!"

Your best friend says, "It's interesting."

Your best friend says, "It's quite boring."

Your best friend says, "It's awful."